# Five Keys

# for

# Understanding Men

## A Woman's Guide

by

Gary L. Malone MD

and Susan Mary Malone

Published by Authorlink Press
An imprint of Authorlink
(http://www.authorlink.com)
755 Laguna .
Irving, Texas 75039-3218, USA

First published by Authorlink Press
An imprint of Authorlink
First Printing, July 1999

Printed in the United States of America

ISBN 978-1-928704-00-3

# CONTENTS

# *Dedication*

"To Sally and Jill, with hopes they come to
understand the men in their lives."
–Gary L. Malone, 1999

"For Gary, my friend as well as brother,
who restored my faith in men."
–Susan Mary Malone

# Introduction
## The Five Golden Keys

*"He's a walking contradiction/Partly truth and partly fiction."*
—Kris Kristofferson

Understanding men—a simple concept. But how would you react to the statement: "Men are easy to understand"? With laughter? Chagrin? Disbelief? For most women, the male mind may as well have been programmed by alien beings.

I have counseled thousands of women. And the most common complaint voiced is, "I can't understand my man's behavior—he's unpredictable, he's erratic." Or, more bluntly, "Testosterone poisoned his brain." As fourteen-year-old Jill Malone put it, "I think, therefore I am not a man."

Answers to questions about husbands, brothers, fathers, and sons however, *do* exist.

It takes two to tango, but men and women arrive at the dance from very different directions. And while one person can neither make nor break a relationship, it helps enormously to comprehend a partner's thought concepts and patterns.

Through the following pages, we will unveil the five hidden keys to the male mind. These keys unlock the locks to the secret of men. By knowing and utilizing them, you can understand (and deal with) over eighty percent of a man's behavior, as well as decipher the motivation behind it.

Sound far-fetched? Men have presented an enigma for women since the time of Adam and Eve. But within closed analytic circles, the mystery called man is well known and well understood. This privileged information, combined with my extensive experience as a psychiatrist and psychoanalyst, will provide *you* with the keys for understanding the men in your midst.

Men's minds work differently than do women's. This is not a news flash. But it is both a biological *and* a psychological phenomenon.

All brains begin female. The presence of a Y chromosome in the fetus, however, means that the developing brain becomes influenced by testosterone, which alters its course. So perhaps the diagnosis of "testosterone poisoning" is not without some merit. In essence, a man's brain is destined to be male from birth, with testosterone playing a vital part in this fate.

Of course, the psychological route of males progresses differently from that of females.

Many strive to explain *how* a man thinks, and how that differs from women's thinking. Doing so provides useful information, but is only part of the story. We will go a step further, showing *why* a man thinks and acts the way he does, which broadens understanding, and makes the *how* a more valuable tool.

Case studies, checklists, workable solutions, and questions and answers follow each chapter, with specific steps for applying the insights to your daily life.

What, then, are these five keys?

Have you ever wondered why men long for relationships, then seem to categorically deny that longing? We will begin by explaining the paradox of *Attachment and Loss*, and how this plays out in men's lives.

Why do men have such a basic need to prove that they are, indeed, men, by engaging in competitive activities and exhibitionistic displays? We will expose *Mastery, Competency, and the Fear of Castration* as motivators behind those behaviors, and show how to discern the healthy actions from the toxic.

From where does all of their guilt come? Their reverent adherence to rules? Understanding the formation of *healthy Guilt* will show the cause, the effect, and how to deal with this in *your* home.

And what about a man's need to be with other men? What is that primitive urge to watch *every single football game, every single weekend*, preferably in the company of *only* other men? Or journey to weekend hunting outings with best buddies, gleeful at the prospect of slaying Bambi's father? Our discussion of the *Need for other Men* will explain this.

How often have you wondered, in complete exasperation, "Why is he so preoccupied with *Sex*?" Men and women come into the sexual arena from very different angles, and we'll explain the role sex plays in a man's mind.

Once you understand the driving forces behind male thinking and acting, an evaluation of your own relationship can be more thoughtfully made. The old adage: "There are no victims in adult relationships, only volunteers," rings as true today as it did for that couple in Eden.

So we'll discuss the *Rule Outs*, and help to identify if he's a stinker *before* investing your whole heart and soul. We'll study the addicted man (how to spot him and what to do about this), and the depressed one. Narcissistic or sociopathic men will become easier to see—the ones who overwhelm you in the beginning with attention and flattery, only to ultimately use you for their own benefit.

Sadistic and abusive men often appear as Prince Charming at first as well. Don't be fooled by this trap. And what is the difference between a healthy sexual appetite versus sexual perversion? A fine but discernible line becomes apparent. What about the traumatized man? Can he ever be a healthy mate?

Finally, we'll talk about *Finding Mr Right*, whether he is still over the horizon, or eating potato chips on your couch. We'll discuss how to determine if adjusting to your man is reasonable or not. In other words, whether to fight, flee, or flow. We'll explain why it is essential to find a man who has a correct balance, and exactly what that balance is. Assuming your man is simply neurotic (most of us are), or healthy (good find!), discovering the five keys will aid enormously in your quest to understand him.

We will also touch on why being alone and facing that aloneness is preferable to remaining in a bad relationship, where old traumas are perpetuated and self-esteem is affected negatively and regularly. In essence, we will discuss ways of wishing more for yourself—how that in this life, you can attain the best relationship possible.

Thoreau said men lead lives of quiet desperation. But desperate for what? And for many men, this desperation is not quiet. Anxiety is pervasive. Demons chase them daily.

In *The Naked Prey*, Cornel Wilde plays a man captured by tribesmen in nineteenth-century South Africa. His friend is killed and he is released, naked and unprotected, into the Savannah to be hunted for sport. He survives by his wits; killing when he has to; running from certain death to unknown safety; meeting his needs along the way.

Men are enraptured by this movie (my wife found it silly) and I often hear men say this is how their lives seem: running for survival, kill or be killed, all but the most basic of needs becoming a luxury. But of what

are men prey? No longer at odds with the
environment, men are now prey to their own fears,
which they pursue with the temerity of bushmen.
Separation, shame, fear of injury, and guilt have
followed men out of the jungle and into their homes
and offices.

Cornel Wilde, for the benefit of those who missed
the movie (ninety percent of all women), finally
makes it to a safe fort with all body parts intact
(whew!). This story encapsulates the elements that
drive men, and those they most fear. Understanding
these drives and fears opens the door to understanding
men.

To the enlightened thinker, information and
understanding provide the keys to happiness. Or, as
his psychiatrist replies to Duane concerning the value
of therapy in Larry McMurtry's *Duane's Depressed*,
"I suppose it depends on what value you place on
understanding, and its power to heal our wounds."
Exploring one's past provides the narrative of how
one arrived here, now. Without understanding, history
is repeated. As William Faulkner said, "The past isn't
over and done with. The past isn't even the past."

Life is compromise. Unconflicted pleasure is
rarely attained. Each person must make peace with his
or her own inner world, as well as negotiate through
external reality to enjoy life. The resulting self-
understanding expands our realm of choices and
possibilities.

For women, comprehending the "other" in their midst heightens not only the viability of relationships, but also pleasure and fulfillment along with self-knowledge. Understanding one's mate is a life-long process. But, as Lao-tse said, "The journey of a thousand miles begins with a single-step."

And this book will light the way.

## Chapter One
# The First Key:
# Attachment and Loss

*To whom I owe this leaping delight*
*That quickens my senses in our waking time*
*And the rhythm that governs the repose of our*
        *Sleeping time,*
        *The breathing in unison*

*Of lovers whose bodies smell of each other*
*Who think the same thoughts without need of speech*
*Who babble the same speech without need*
        *of meaning...*
        —T .S. Eliot, "A Dedication to My Wife."

*Or:*
*"I would do anything for love."*
—Meat Loaf

## ATTACHMENT

The most intense experiences in life are wordless. As a psychiatrist and psychoanalyst, I spend much of my time transcribing the indescribable—trying to make sense of that deep well filled with swirling, fluid feelings. Feelings that to one degree or another, we *all* have.

More than three centuries ago, John Donne said, "No man is an island." An ageless truth. Nor can man stand alone, at least not for long. We are interdependent beings and *need* our connections for emotional as well as physical survival. But why?

Whether outwardly apparent or not, *all* men feel an intense longing and need to attach. Terms such as "commitment-phobic," and "men who can't love," leave the impression that many of today's men desire an isolated, separate life.

If such a man exists, I don't know him, nor even *of* him. Our first and most intense drive is to merge. For at his very core, man's most primary need is for attachment. This hunger in man's heart has its beginning in infancy, and is sustained in varying forms throughout his lifetime. It is, quite simply, the longing to merge with She-Who-Is-Love.

A human being's most intense experiences occur during the first years of his life. If, as Jewish theologian Martin Buber says, "...in fetal existence, we were in communion with the universe," in infancy we were in communion with our primary love object, otherwise known as Mother.

During the first months of life, we are utterly unaware of the existence of an*other* human presence. However, by the second month, our shuttight universe expands and we merge with Mother, forming a dual unity with one boundary. Whether or not Mother proves capable of mothering is immaterial. Merging occurs. It is our very first experience of awareness. We spend the remainder of our days attempting to recreate this unconflicted union.

Jung refers to this as a time of union with the collective "Earth Mother" in all of us—whom we share with our worldly birth mother. The Freudians speak of the "oceanic bliss" felt during these first months, providing a pleasure in merging that is forever longed for but irreplaceable.

But what, for god's sakes, does an infant's development have to do with the now grown man's actions?

Plenty.

The first experience we have with our mothers provides the template for *all* future relationships. This experience is deep-rooted, intense, largely unconscious, and unfortunately, wordless.

For the first months of life, the bonding experience is actually a matter of life and death. Researchers noted that in post World War II nurseries, the infants who attached to a caregiver lived. Those who did not—even with adequate nutrition and physical care—died. "Failure to thrive" is the term for dying from lack of love.

This syndrome has its adult counterpart as well. Our folklore and family histories often tell of a husband dying within a year of his wife's burial. Though surrounded by a loving family, he has lost *the* love, *the* attachment, that sustained him. "Failure to thrive" can occur at any age. The infant's attachment to the mothering object also proves necessary later in life. If the template for relationships is never set, healthy bonding becomes difficult if not impossible to learn as an adult. In other words, mature, loving relationships don't happen. This "attachment behavior" not only aids in psychological development, it predicts a good outcome for all adult relationships, including therapy. I.e., a person needs the ability to attach to a therapist for successful treatment, and in order to relate to other people as well.

In the Harlowe's Monkeys studies, male primates separated from their mothers at birth showed a pronounced inability to later accept a mate. In fact, if separated from their mothers too early, many male monkeys were unable to breed at all.

Jane Goodall has spent much of her lifetime studying chimpanzees. While researching the mother /child relationship, Goodall found this most intense bond to be the continuous thread throughout chimps' lives. If, in fact, the mother was killed or captured before an offspring passed infancy (two years or so), the infant wasted away—even if care was available. These infants became depressed, quit eating, and died.

The cry of "But we're not apes!" arises here, and of course, this is true. All primates, however, share the need to attach as a primary drive. And though basic needs become obscured in humans by questions of morals, ethics, and analysis, the drives nonetheless exist in basically unaltered states.

So, from the earliest experiences in this life, we are all bonded both physically and emotionally to Mother. Never underestimate the power of this bond. Judith Viorst, in her groundbreaking psychological work about what must be 'given up to grow up,' *Necessary Losses*, recounts the story of a young boy lying in a hospital bed:

"He is frightened and in pain. Burns cover forty percent of his small body. Someone has doused him with alcohol and then, unimaginably, has set him on fire. He cries for his mother. His mother has set him on fire."

The desire to merge remains with us, unaltered, through the entirety of our lives.

Remember the opening and closing scenes to the movie, *Citizen Kane*? The emphasis on, and quest to uncover, the meaning of "Rosebud"? John Foster Kane had it all: wealth, power, fame. Surrounded by meaningless things, he died alone in the vain attempt to "hold onto" something he could not grasp. His final thoughts floated to a snowy, idyllic blur connected to an early childhood experience of warmth and joy (snow often represents mother's milk in Freudian dream analysis). The sled from Kane's childhood bore the name, "Rosebud."

So men live in quiet desperation for what? Sex, domination, and freedom from guilt hold their power, but at the beginning and end of life, men long for the "oceanic bliss" of mother's milk.

No man truly wants to be an island. This longing to merge is a basic drive, and in no way negates masculinity. It merely *is*.

## SEPARATION

This desire for oneness, however, does not continue in an unconflicted manner. Soon, the process of separation and the quest for autonomy (self-hood) begin. As the saying goes, "A ship in a harbor is safe, but that's not what ships are for." Herein springs the primordial struggle for life—the push/pull with the mothering object.

As already stated, the infant cannot distinguish between the self and mother. Any parent can elicit a "social smile" if the baby is approached in a nonthreatening way. At about eight months, however, a hallmark occurs that forever changes a being's perception of itself and the world: other beings can be recognized as strangers. Mother and I are separate and there can only be one out there Who-is-She. *Separation Anxiety* (the signal fear that forewarns the loss of the object—Mother) remains constant through-out life. It becomes a permanent part of our psyches.

As the infant begins to explore both the external world *and* internal perceptions, psychological growth continues, paralleling physical development and mastery. But the early view is very myopic.

The infant's mind can only experience the good, loving Mother, *or* the bad, punishing Mother. The infant can only experience *one or the other*—Mother is either all loving or all punishing. At about the age of four, in normal development, the child can "fuse" the good and bad images of Mother into one whole person.

This ability to fuse the positive and negative aspects of mother remains with us throughout our lifetimes, and carries over into all relationships. Under duress, however, we may again transiently experience the world as all good or all bad.

Mythology is often referred to as the collective unconscious of a culture. This is the innermost part of the psyche, which is not readily accessible to the conscious mind, but is ostensibly shared by everyone through symbols and archetypes. A common motif in myths is the Dangerous Goddess—the bliss-bestowing goal of the hero's quest. She is, according to the noted mythologist Joseph Campbell:

"...the incarnation of the promise of perfection; the soul's assurance that, at the conclusion of its exile in a world of organized inadequacies, the bliss that once was known will be known again...."

She is the womb and the tomb, uniting the "good" and the "bad" mothers. Again, these must be ultimately fused for mature relationships to occur.

Much criticism has been levied at modern Disney movies, where the mothers are usually absent or evil.

This heightens the anxiety in children, their worst fears realized, and in fact adds to the relief of the ultimate resolution in all Disney movies. *The Lion King* deviated from this, portraying the "good" mother in existence, allowing the conflict to emerge between the "good" father and "bad" uncle. But both good and bad aspects *must* be present within an individual's psyche to provide healthy functioning.

In certain character disorders, these objects fail to fuse (see Chapter Six), leaving a child without the skill to evoke a "complete" image of mother, resulting in disastrous consequences. We need the calming, reassuring-but-firm mother with us always. Kane's mother remained with him, albeit quiescently, until she returned to be with him at the moment of death.

This, too, is common. During the most frightening experiences in life the wish to be "one" becomes overt and can be said aloud. Michael Elliot described the scene on Omaha Beach, D-Day:

"...Many were so scared that they lost control of their bladders and bowels ...Many men cried, many called their mothers."

To the adult as well as the child, the push/pull remains a constant. From the ages of two to four, a child begins to push out and experience the world. The need to attach becomes mixed with the desire to gain mastery over his or her world; to separate; to become an individual. An oscillation occurs, a refueling, as the child moves from mother to outer experience and back again. Up until this point, males and females develop, in psychological terms, roughly along the same path.

But after sex differences become evident (ages two to four), and with the onset of the Oedipal Phase (ages four to six, and about which we'll discuss in depth in chapters Two and Three), the parallels cease. Simply put, the Oedipal Phase is that time when the normal child's feelings for the opposite-sex parent become romantic or sexual. When resolved in a healthy manner, this transient phase then leads to the next stages of growth.

During this time, however, separation from the parent plays out differently as per girls and boys. Girls must separate from their primary love object (Mom), but still relate to her in order to regulate identity. A girl must suddenly view herself as separate from Mother, while identifying with her as both a female, and a rival!

For a boy at this stage, however, phallic pre-occupation heightens. His desires for Mom change. She becomes a romanticized object. So although a boy must separate from Mom to be masculine, he still desires the same object (unlike the girl). A boy never leaves the primary love object, the *aim* just changes. Of course, he must later substitute other objects.

So the longing for merger hasn't left him, it has just taken a different form. The desire to recoup his loss of attachment to Mother—his Original Loss—remains a driving force within: the drive to again merge and be one.

After the Oedipal Phase comes a brief reprieve known as Latency. During this time, we see a temporary lull with regards to deeper psychosexual development. Although a relative term in that six-to-twelve-year-olds are not exactly quiet, at least the intense phases of human development get a respite. Here, "pseudo" autonomy is set up as boys interact with other boys. The real beginning or separateness comes with the teenage years.

Adolescence, young adulthood, and adulthood (up to age thirty-five) are dominated in men's minds with thoughts of autonomy, career definitions, triumphs, and sex. The sex drive, placed within men to insure perpetuation of the species, overwhelms men's psychic lives. Still, the need to stay connected to family and friends, the pursuit of career identity, and separation/individuation issues remain present though undergoing changes. The need for attachment, however, *never* abates.

During the adolescent years, this need may be hard to recognize. The sexual drive heats up. Separation from parents becomes paramount. Throughout development and into adult life, the need to attach may take the form of a transitional object—a symbolic representative of the longed-for blissful state. This can be a thing (car, stereo, baseball mitt), a place (elementary school, "My" room), or a time (sophomore year at the Deke house). This grounds men and evokes the positive feeling of oneness.

The object-love often continues into adulthood. Roy Rogers had such an attachment to his horse that he had the animal stuffed after its death, to forever stand in his living room (God only knows what Dale really thought of this). Attaching to a thing, time, or place is much easier, psychologically speaking, than attaching to a person. Of course, it is also *much* less gratifying. Successful attachment to another person allows one to enjoy the physical and emotional payoffs of a friend, companion, lover, and (hopefully) co-parent, which can be tremendously rewarding (as well as difficult and anxiety producing). This doesn't happen with inanimate objects. But moving from adolescent object love into adult attachment to a woman requires some growth.

As a male's development progresses, this longing for merger becomes more threatening than it does for a woman. It represents the loss of hard-won autonomy. It represents loss of function and manhood, which will be dealt with further in Chapter Two.

But again: though the need to attach may be feared and denied, it exists nevertheless in the minds of all men.

The fact that most men marry attests to this. In the midst of erotic fantasies and the quest for multiple sex partners, most men marry in their twenties and thirties. Marriage is the ascension of man's need for attachment—to be loved—over the sex drive.

At mid-life, as the sex drive wanes and careers solidify, men become even more attached. This can create a welcomed partner for a woman, or can be experienced as a whiny wimp. Here, men become more comfortable, less threatened by their own needs, and can allow themselves more closeness.

An ominous occurrence at this time is the dreaded mid-life crisis where faced with diminishing physical and sexual powers, and seeing "the end of the tunnel," men regress to more adolescent coping styles of macho behaviors. This may include sexual adventures (invariably with younger women), or more significant, a decision to change careers, which is usually a way of avoiding conflicts over career choice (selling coconuts on the beach at St. Thomas, for instance). A healthy "taking stock" should occur at this time. To differentiate the healthy from the not, check if the aforementioned sexy young woman is involved (the acid test for mid-life decisions).

For men over fifty and on into later life and old age, attachment to a woman becomes of paramount importance. Even Hugh Hefner, the icon of American bachelorhood, finally gave in and married (following a stroke!). Perhaps only the advent of Viagra put him back on the market. Though parents die and children leave, a life-mate can remain constant.

This actually becomes a matter of life and death to a man, as single men die much more quickly from all causes than do married ones. Even more ominous, unemployed, single men over fifty who drink comprise the group at greatest risk for suicide. For males facing the loss of potency without a woman, death is often preferable.

As men age and approach death, phallic needs to dominate recede. Men overwhelmingly ask to be buried next to their wives or mothers! The notable exception to this is soldiers interred in war cemeteries, such as George S. Patton, buried in the third Army cemetery in Luxembourg. For these men, this bonding proved the most intense and won out over maternal connections (this will be more fully discussed in Chapter Four). Still, it portrays the undying drive to merge.

## DENIAL

How often have you seen men deny their need to attach? When they do, don't buy it. See it instead for what it is—*his desire to deny.*

This denial stems from one, or a combination of, the many internal conflicts with which men struggle. In other words, a negation is as good as an affirmation, as whatever appears to be true on the surface is linked to an opposite truth beneath the surface.

Denial of attachment is often the attempt to avoid separation anxiety by denying we ever were attached (and therefore, never need to separate). Sometimes the Original Attachment and Loss were so painful or distorted, a man deals with the whole experience by denying it. Unfortunately, that in no way negates the reality of the events, nor lessens their hold on him. As Freud said, "There is no negative in the unconscious."

As a good example of this, John Grady Cole in Cormac McCarthy's *All The Pretty Horses* sets out on his quest for manhood after the family farm is lost. Years earlier his mother had abandoned both husband and child. And before his adventure can rightfully begin, Cole searches for his mother. He sees her from a distance, but she remains unavailable. He leaves without making contact. In Mexico, he faces great trials with courage and honor, but the defining parameters surround his love for a beautiful woman. A woman who is and remains unavailable.

Continued longing for the mothering object leads to Cole's ultimate demise in *Cities of the Plains*. Our hero's longing was never fulfilled—a common motif when the original loss is never resolved.

In healthy men, separation anxiety is counter-balanced by the drive for mastery and satisfaction in other areas. Thus, most men leave home. Cole did so, but only after home was lost.

Home, however, never really leaves us, and is a given throughout life. We first ask of a new acquaintance, "So, where're you from?" Even the adventurous, interplanetary explorer, ET, once separated from the "mother ship" had but one wish: Phone Home.

The degree of this home leaving is determined by the individual's sense of self. A man fearful of the anxiety surrounding competition in adult life may become a "homeboy" and be uncomfortable away from "homebase."

The story is told of Henry David Thoreau, whose mother suggested upon his graduation from Harvard that he put his belongings in a knapsack and travel the world. Young Thoreau dissolved into a fit of tears, thinking that his mother was sending him away from her. And, away from home.

Other objects substitute for home, with teary-eyed visits to the "Alma Mater" or homeland (Mother Russia). Under stress of illness or failure, the need to return home surfaces, whether in a literal or metaphoric ("back to basics") sense. Death raises anxieties at all levels, but separation from loved ones is always paramount. Thus, elaborate preparations are made to diminish anxiety, usually to little avail. In spite of the intense drive to seek out and conquer new territories, few men travel far from home.

Even Thoreau, the Transcendentalist, finally did depart to a hut he built in the woods of Walden Pond, to expound upon the solitary, self-reliant life. However, he built his cabin a mere mile from his mother's house, and returned there to visit her. Every day.

And those who do leave come back, if only symbolically. In J.R.R. Tolkein's *Lord of the Rings* trilogy, our heroes killed dragons, countless orcs and sorcerers, participated in the triumph of good over evil, only to return home to their beloved shrine. Ultimately, they went to Gray Havens, a land "east of the sun and west of the moon" for blissful eternity—sounding substantially akin to "mother's milk." As the narrator in Robert Penn Warren's *All the King's Men* put it, "I had come home. I was the thing that always came back."

In rites of passage from adolescence to adulthood, however, a man must release "childish" attachments to move into the conflicted arena of heterosexual relationships. There is usually an oscillation that may play out over many years and be held onto in adult life ("Don't throw out my bowling trophy!"). Our hero in *All The Pretty Horses* is willing to leave Mexico without the woman he loves, but not without his horse!

In order to truly enter adulthood, each man must overcome his fear of women to attach. Again, denial of the need for attachment appears. He may fear his loss of competence due to relinquishing some of his phallic conquests. He may be afraid of guilt associated with "capturing" and merging with the love object (symbolic Mother). Unconscious retaliation from the father and therefore castration cannot be far behind (see Chapter Two). The *wish*, according to Freud, is at the core. But it is followed by the fear that in getting the wish, calamity follows. Freud said that all through life, feelings and behaviors are direct expressions of a drive, or sublimations of a drive, *or* a reaction against a drive.

In *Lonesome Dove*, Woodrow F. Call, a man-who-needs-no-woman, has his only romantic relationship with a whore. He denies this, however, even denying the evidence of the union—his son. Throughout the story, Call refuses to speak the woman's name, negating her existence. A negation is as good as an affirmation....

Men generally lack conscious awareness of their wish to attach, and harbor an unconscious fear of falling into the bottomless pit of the *need* to be close ("Tar Baby" fear of being sucked into a suffocating substance). In effect, they feel smothered.

Men also fear attaching too strongly—associating this with Mommy's Boy designations, and the loss of manhood. A man who has over-attached will be quite comfortable in his marriage. Unfortunately, he will be unable to perform in bed.

And finally, he may fear the loss of autonomy—for which he has struggled so hard all of his life. Autonomy is a universal quest and is sexless—it is the sense of self one has as a self-actualized, independent person. Men speak of the role of separation as it defines and empowers the self, helping them to achieve that all-important sense of mastery. The need to attach can threaten this.

As men's wishes to be cared for and merge are often unconscious, their expression may be seen in other ways. Adult men often subtly (or not so subtly) complain to women about their health or life status, when they would *never* consider complaining to men. To complain to other men carries a different meaning; it presents as non-threatening; it is a way of asking for "quarter," or mercy, which carries with it a whole host of other meanings (Chapter Two discusses this further).

Men often experience psychosomatic illnesses, or become hypochondriacs late in life when it becomes acceptable to be taken care of. More often men moan to women with the hopes of being nurtured ("don't worry, it's okay"). A degree of this is tolerable and even healthy, but it can get in the way of self-care (a healthy man *can* nurture himself) and be infantilizing. Such a man is more likely to develop real illnesses with negative health consequences.

More benign manifestations of this need to attach often surface as well, as in the oft-repeated slogan: "The way to a man's heart is through his stomach." Indeed, this is one of the sayings the feminists warn is a masculine plot—an offshoot of phallocentric culture. Unfortunately, the latter is true. But so is the former—even armies, as Napoleon said, "travel on their stomachs."

Men not only like to eat, but especially, they like to be fed. This "oral" experience is the first and often the most consistently blissful early experience with Mother.

For many men, a woman cooking for them is gratifying in its own right. This returns them to warm and safe times, when every need was met. While camping or roughing it, men eat (not quiche) but beans and jerky (while simultaneously longing for a woman to cook!). Survivors of World War II POW camps say they kept themselves going with shared fantasies of food from home (hot buttered pancakes took first place). One man carried a sandwich on his person for fifty years, until his death, so as to never have the fear of starvation visited upon him again.

Often stories of war contain romantic subplots between the hero and his nurse. In Robert Flynn's *The Last Klick*, an injured war correspondent awakens to find his nurse has brought supper.

"I brought you something to eat," she said. "You may forget someone who stops you from bleeding to death but you never forget someone who feeds you."

"You're right," he said. "Everyone remembers their mother."

A man condemned to die does not receive a last fling, or a last home-run, but a last meal (mine would be my wife's homemade chicken soup). The calming connection to bliss eases the passage into the unknown.

*Mable's Kitchen, Fort Worth, Texas:*

*Fried chicken, rice with brown gravy. A simple meal, but served in "my spot" at the kitchen table. The feeling this causes is not reproducible in the known world.*

*My mother's love is passed to me through her secret deep-fried batter. I draw strength from her glow and the warmth of her kitchen. Always. (Pass the gravy, please.)*

This concept *can* be overdone, however. Remember, over-gratification of one drive can lead to suppression of another, so use discretion!

For a fortunate few, your man actually cooks, not just for himself but for you too. If this can be done without the cost of masculinity, count your lucky stars and enjoy.

Hot tubs, saunas, and lazy-boys are all regressive pulls back to connections with Mom. "Regression: the service of the ego" is an adaptive skill that is not only useful but needed. Anyone who has sat in an oval tub at or above body temperature, floating mindlessly, can attest to the reliving of a womb-like state where all troubles drift away.

Rock music appears to be rebellious—driving the adolescent or young adult from his home and into the world. Lyrics (not of love songs) portray emancipation and freedom. Conversely, however, most rock songs have at their heart a "one-two" beat which, if separated, has almost the same rhythm as a maternal heartbeat. Remember the "womb-bear"— the stuffed toy for infants that gave a shushy, one-two cadence, calming babies in their cribs? Increased bass, vibrating down to the toes, provides the same effect. Mick Jagger is really a mama's boy.

This longing for the merger of the womb-like state is pervasive and forever. How close is our lead-in poem "...the rhythm that governs the repose of our sleeping time/The breathing in unison/of lovers whose bodies smell of each other/ Who think the same thoughts without need of speech/And babble the same speech without need of meaning..." to Mother/womb, Mother/infant?

Men also bolster their denial through obsessive thoughts and compulsive behavior. This drives most women batty. The tinkering with the lawnmower or water heater seems endless (but handy!), however, it serves an important function for men. It reinforces competence *and* avoids having more conflicted issues (dependence upon you!) emerge into conscious awareness. Many a man, if suddenly unable to obsess or tinker, becomes anxious or depressed. On the whole, you're better off with a "Honey Do" list, and patience.

Men have other ways of keeping things out of awareness, but none so powerful or prevalent as denial and obsessive/compulsive behaviors. Some men become aesthetics, denying all needs (monks). Some internalize (i.e., write books) or find ways to sublimate unmet needs to get partial gratification. *Healthy* men use humor as a way of interacting with women as well as discharging psychic energies and avoiding confrontation. By learning your mate's style, you can anticipate his actions.

For as Erich Fromm put it so well in *The Art of Loving*:

"Man is gifted with reason; he is *life being aware of itself*; he has awareness of himself, of his fellow man, of his past, and of the possibilities of his future. This awareness of himself as a separate entity, the awareness of his own short life span, of the fact that without his will he is born and against his will he dies, that he will die before those whom he loves, or they before him, the awareness of his aloneness and separateness, of his helplessness before the forces of nature and of society, all this makes his separate, disunited existence an unbearable prison. He would become insane could he not liberate himself from this prison and reach out, unite...."

# CASE STUDY

*"Mother, Mother Ocean/I have heard your call."*
—Jimmy Buffett

Priscilla and Jerry

Priscilla, a successful professional woman in her thirties, came to her first session stunned. Her fiancé was going "back home" to North Carolina, leaving her confused and abandoned.

Jerry, also in his thirties, worked in the same profession. He had arrived in Dallas from the Old South, to take advantage of an unusual career opportunity.

They seemed the ideal couple—both successful in the same profession, old enough not to be blinded by love, and age-appropriate.

Priscilla and Jerry felt an instant attraction, dated, and planned to wed. Then, inexplicably, Jerry's trips home became more frequent. He finally said, "Whenever I get on the plane bound for Dallas, I cry." Ultimately, Jerry resigned his job, broke off the engagement, and moved back home.

"It must be me," Priscilla said, fighting to maintain composure. "If I were enough, *good* enough, he'd stay."

Priscilla had personalized the loss as being due to her own flaw.

As we painfully walked through the relationship and Priscilla's own history, we discovered the source of her "flaw"—her strong sense that her father favored her older sister and that her mother, while seeming to love her, didn't really *like* her. She had fought a lifetime battle to be "good enough."

These kinds of internal conflicts surface in deeply emotional relationships. And while Priscilla's sense of unworthiness caused her concern, it wasn't the culprit in their futile engagement.

The relationship brought Jerry's longing for home to the surface. This is, in fact, an extraordinarily common phenomenon for a man in his first serious pairing. Jerry, an energetic and apparently brilliant man, experienced his *first* attempt to separate from home by moving to Dallas. The pull of Mom and Home overpowered his struggle for autonomy, and for this relationship.

The second of three children and the only boy, Jerry experienced minimal conflicts with his passive father. He was, however, the apple of his mother's eye. He excelled at sports and school and advanced rapidly in his profession. He had previous girlfriends, but could always be found "at home." He connected with other men, but this overcompetitiveness limited the depth of the friendships.

Jerry, in classic macho style, had denied his attachment to home and only when the reality of separation was felt by his commitment to Priscilla could his veneer be punctured, and his true feelings emerge. In the end, he could not let go and leave home.

Could this painful end have been predicted?

Psychoanalysis is said to be like fortune telling—but in reverse. We expertly predict the past; the future remains more difficult.

Though Jerry had shown those good signs of stability—professional training, ability to move and work at a distant site, and apparent emotional depth—he also exhibited macho behavior. He carried a defensive chip on his shoulder, readily readable to all who met him.

A mature man does not need to be overtly macho—when the chips are down we will *all* get to show our cards. No preview is needed. This sort of behavior belies a fear. And the content of that fear will fall, within a high probability, into attachment, castration, or guilt.

Jerry feared all, but separation turned out to be the most powerful.

In this line of work, you can't *know* something until you know it. However, as the philosopher Soren Kierkegaard said, "Life can only be understood backwards, but it must be lived forwards." And in our studies, reasonable predictors can still be made by surface behavior. Priscilla's suspicions should have been peaked by Jerry's overly aggressive manner, and by the fact that he was a bit old to just now be leaving home. Otherwise, few clues jumped out.

In essence, Jerry's earliest dependency needs on his mother had never been relinquished. He had generalized to his immediate surroundings ("Home"), but never made the difficult psychological move to detach from Mother, then experience himself as a separate, autonomous person, and only then reinvest in another relationship. He could not trust to release his pacifier with the hopes that the real world could offer greater gratifications. If Jerry had been able to make that jump, there would likely still be trouble as his true sense of selfhood was not developed— his machismo was a facade.

Jerry's choice actually saved Priscilla some grief as the likely scenario would have been an extreme attachment to her with the strong need to deny this attachment. The results would have been manifested in the acting out of independent behavior—pushing away, a possible affair, *anything* to deny the attachment; or hostile/dependency—the resentful bashing of the needed one. Priscilla learned from the experience, and used her knowledge to choose more wisely.

## SOLUTIONS

Though a man may claim to "long for his freedom," the primary motivator to pull away comes from feeling emasculated, or from a sense of guilt, with perhaps a reactionary fear of being smothered. *Don't!*

Remember, John Wayne, Clint Eastwood, and Sean Connery all attached (sometimes several times) without losing their manhood. Allow space. But also consider what you know about your man's need to attach—a need he likely does not know about himself. And though he shares this need with other primates, *we*, as humans, can be aware of why.

You must also be aware of the differences between healthy commitment and investment vs. dependency. Co-dependence is the popular term for someone who regulates self-esteem through attachment to other people. The psychiatric joke goes: You can diagnose a co-dependent if someone else's life passes before his eyes when he falls off a cliff. Basically, if you never separate to the point of feeling yourself as a capable and whole person, you may attempt to fill these inadequacies with other persons or objects (John Grady Cole and his horse).

Healthy individuals can function and even live independently. A relationship adds depth and greater gratification to one's life. A commitment to "forsake all others" allows a level of trust to develop in order to experience closeness, *hopefully* without losing the boundary of who you are. Dependency (or co-dependency) occurs when that person is *needed* for one to feel whole or complete.

It takes some skill to recognize the difference. But healthy attachment centers on your man's ability to invest in you without losing himself or needing to deny the investment. You must learn to read this accurately to avoid Priscilla's mistake.

A healthy man can fall in love. He can invest emotionally, psychologically, and financially in you while continuing to be who he is. You must do your part by allowing him the freedom to develop his own personality while being attached to you. If, however, you become everything to him, occupying his every thought, he has crossed over into dependency. This may be experienced as needy "gloppiness," a strong desire to control your actions, or a defensive denial of the need. You must keep your own boundaries while assessing where your man falls in this spectrum:

> _____ >

| Gloppy | Healthy | Island |
|--------|---------|--------|
| (needy) | (able to attach) | (denies closeness) |

- Expect an emotionally healthy man to attach. If after a reasonable time he is still distant, other issues may be involved.

- Don't force a man to commit too early. Men fear the power of their dependency needs, and may bolt.
- On the other hand, don't wait too long to broach commitment. After an appropriate amount of time, let him know your feelings, and expect an answer. Timing is everything.
- You don't need to be the only important person in his life. Friends and family play necessary roles, but your place is special.
- Attachment builds slowly with men, but tends to remain. Nurture his loyalty—don't fight it.

# CHECKLIST
# UNHEALTHY ATTACHMENT:

1). Does he seem to be overly attached to his mother, hometown, or car (horse), to the point of negating you? "Overly" meaning he must see or talk with his mother daily, or constantly talks of moving back home, etc.

2). Does he deny all attachment—overtly viewing himself as a "lone wolf" in the world?

3). Has he let go of home only to overly attach to you, either overtly *or* covertly (and deny it)?

4). When you "baby" him, does he seem more childlike, fussy, and less manly? He may be regressively using you as his new mother.

5). Does he have no connection with his past (friends, home, school)? This is a clear indicator of denial.

6). Does he feel threatened or jealous when you spend time away with *your* friends?

7). Has he become more needy and dependent as your relationship has progressed?

*Gary L. Malone MD
And Susan Mary Malone*

# CHECKLIST
# HEALTHY ATTACHMENT:

1). Has he detached without anger from his mother? His home? But can still maintain a reasonable relationship with them? This is a sign of healthy autonomy.

2). Can he see his mother as a person in her own right, as opposed to merely his mother?

3). Is he not only aware but also accepting of his need for you in his life, without being overly dependent?

4). Can he be away from you, and while missing you, carry on successfully with the rest of his life?

5). When he connects with his friends from childhood, is the experience positive?

6). Does he maintain his adult friendships?

7). Does he seem to have an adult-like relationship with his parents, a good balance of friendship, a strong sense of self, and can attach to you while maintaining autonomy? Then you might not *really* need this book!

# QUESTIONS AND ANSWERS

1). Question: My husband is twenty-five, stable, and I know he loves me. He seems to attach to me, then goes off in search of *something*, and stays gone. Does he get tired of me, or do I not give him what he needs?

Answer: You may be personalizing something that has little to do with you. Your husband's need to be separate may be a denial of his attachment to you, but could simply be healthy autonomy. "What he needs" may be both attachment *and* autonomy. Regardless, his need to be separate does not mean you are not enormously important.

2). Question: Whenever my husband and I fight, he immediately retreats to the garage to work on his car. I feel abandoned. How can this behavior have anything to do with attachment?

Answer: It is likely that when you fight, your husband feels a risk that you will abandon *him*. It sounds as if he uses obsessive/compulsive defenses combined with denial to compensate—his style for keeping conflicts out of awareness. *Allow him time*, then calmly state your concerns.

3). Question: When is denial a true answer, and when is it just denial?

Answer: The emotion involved in the denial will tell you if it is an untrue statement, or is in fact true and the denial is unacceptable. Ex:

"You have blue hair." "No, I don't." A correct and true denial.

"You are acting scared." "Like hell I am!" He doth protest too much.

4). Question: If I know he's in denial, what do I do?

Answer: Attempt to approach him in a calm, non-threatening manner with your concerns. Respect the defense as protecting him from intense discomfort, but don't *you* deny reality, to yourself or him either one. He must then work with the information you provide—you can't do it for him.

5). Question: If men have such a strong need to attach, why do so many married men (seventy-five percent) have affairs—even those who say their marriages are happy?

The answer lies in the innate biology and psychology of men. Sex is more intense for men and does more inter-psychically. An affair reinforces manhood by denying castration and attachment, while providing sexual satisfaction. This will be more fully addressed in chapters two and five.

6). Question: What of the man who goes running every time his mother calls. How do you deal with this situation?

Answer: First, understand what the motivator really is. Then, if these situations interfere with your relationship, be prepared to gently confront him. Do not expect him to "give up" his mother, but insist that his investment to *you* be primary.

7). Or the man who proclaims to "hate his mother"?

Answer: See if there is a realistic reason to support this—sexual, physical, or emotional abuse. If not, this is but a sign of emotional immaturity— the need to *hate* to separate. Keep looking: he likely someday will hate you.

8). Or is cold and distant towards her?

Answer: Ditto.

9). Question: My husband is fifty, and though he has always proclaimed to have hated the town in which he grew up, now he speaks of it with almost reverence, and longs to go back. Why did this change?

Answer: It never changes, it is simply now entering conscious awareness. This could of course represent a regression in response to life changes, but otherwise, represents an acceptance of ending the attachment to this phase of life. If "longs to go back" turns into concrete plans to move, ask for a rational reappraisal. A friendly hint from you might actually be welcomed.

10). Question: My husband, always so active and athletic, now just sits in front of the tube and gets fatter. What happened?

Answer: He has regressed in the face of external or internal conflicts, *or* been gratified by you. Remind him in a non-threatening way, of the man you fell in love with, along with the fact that your ideal love partner is not a couch potato.

11). Question: He seems irritable with me most of the time, while I seem to be his only friend. It's really his pride that's suffering—all his setbacks at work. Why does he blame me?

Answer: In the face of stress, he is likely projecting blame onto the only stationary target (you!), or irritated with you for not nurturing him well enough to solve the problem—either way placing unreasonable burdens upon you. Do not accept blame if it is not your fault—it's bad for you *and* him. This may bring overt conflict, but gives an opportunity for a healthier reaction. In essence, by speaking up, you provide him with a reality check.

12). Question: I give my husband everything I can—love, comfort, food—and he seems appreciative. When it's "my time" in the bedroom, he seems like a little boy! I'm frustrated.

Answer: Infantilizing a man will encourage him to behave like an infant. Have reasonable, adult expectations of him (even in bed), and don't let your "need to nurture" take away his manhood.

13). Question: My husband is such a slob! He constantly leaves newspapers and even beer cans lying on the floor. He'll leave his underwear in the middle of the bedroom. I've even had to talk with him about his bathroom habits—why can't he hit the pot?

Answer: Your husband is displaying "anal regressive behavior," which is a way of enjoying soiling with the expectation that *you* clean up after him. Inform him that his mother does not reside with you, and to clean up after himself. *Don't* encourage this behavior by picking up after him.

14). Question: My man is still dependent upon his mother. Can he simply transfer those needs to me?

Answer: The case of Jerry and Priscilla provides that answer. Jerry's denial and his macho behavior helped him cover his attachments to Mother and Home, and *keep* them unconscious. He only became aware of the intensity of his feelings when faced with the reality of separating from Mom to invest in Priscilla. He was unable to "switch" because his dependency on his mother and home were too intense, too primitive, *and* previously unaddressed.

Had Jerry been consciously aware of these needs for the preceding ten or so years, he could have "left home" in a more tolerable, step-wise fashion. Conscious awareness through introspection, reality testing, or therapy would have helped Jerry (*and* Priscilla). Perhaps in his next relationship, Jerry can make the break.

Are your man's dependency needs conscious? Much of the answer lies here. If not, the end result may very well be as in Priscilla's case. And, as in her situation, the result would prove fortunate. For attachment such as Jerry's carries all the romantic appeal of a leech.

15). Question: I want my husband to attach and invest in me, but how do I ensure it doesn't become out-right dependence?

Answer: In the end, it is all a question of balance. If he attaches to you, then you become an integral part of his life—physically and psychologically. But he must not lose who he is. Dependency occurs when he no longer experiences himself as a complete person without you. If this occurs, he will likely deny the dependency or attempt to manipulate you in an effort to modulate his own fears.

To foster the right balance, it is essential that you are centered—enjoying his presence, but not needing it to be whole. Insist on him prioritizing you, but encourage him to invest in his career, hobbies, and other men to maintain his sense of autonomy. Expect him to behave like a grown-up and a man. If you become Mother, the expectation that you will take care of him exists in his mind. Worse, no woman enjoys being a "Mother" to his "boy" in bed. Know clearly who you are and what you want and say it to him in terms he can understand.

*Chapter Two*

# The Second Key: Mastery, Competency, and the Fear of Castration

*"Where am I now that I really need me?"* —
Anonymous

## THE NON-MORTAL WOUND

Men's psyches are wrapped up in their anatomies. Or, as Sam Keene says so well in *Fire in the Belly*, "...a boy's penis becomes the pole around which his consciousness revolves."

How often have you pondered (or cursed) this fact over the course of your life? Women become painfully aware of men's phallic fascination early on, and though the behavioral tendencies of this phenomenon change over time, the root fears and psychic needs remain constant. So, from where or what do these needs and fears stem?

In a word, *anatomy*.

Once the boy passes through the attachment and separation phases, his development progresses into awareness not only of "other," but also of the *differences* of other. Men's genitalia are external and exposed (vulnerable). Seeing a woman (usually Mother) without a penis affirms the boy's fear of losing his. As Freud said, "…the child (male) arrives at the discovery that the penis is not a possession which is common to all creatures like himself …Anatomy is destiny."

And a male's anatomy has a focal point, which is quite different from what females experience. Phyllis Tyson, a contemporary psychoanalyst and theorist, put the difference most eloquently by pointing out that a woman's anatomy allows her to experience her *whole* body as a sexual entity, while men's sexual and psychic lives center around the penis.

So the boy becomes "wrapped around" his penis about the time he realizes that since not everybody has one, the possibility must exist that his can be lost. Thus begins the lifelong drama of protecting one's anatomy, denying castration through phallic displays (penis-measuring contests), and seeking to attain *competence*—the mature outcome. Throughout life, this mastery and competence become a male's chief defense against the fear of losing his most vital parts.

*Castration.* The word sends chills down the spines of men. I once saw a man refuse orchiectomy (the surgical removal of the testicles) as a treatment for advanced prostate cancer—his only chance for survival.

"What kind of life would that be," he said painfully. "I wouldn't even be a man."

As a boy I watched the young bulls being turned into steers on my father's ranch. "Ouch," I whispered involuntarily.

"Hell," the wrangler said, "I'd as soon be hamburger if that 'us me."

The value men place on their penises and testicles influences all areas of their lives. The very word testify literally means, "I swear by my testicles." (The reason women could not "testify" in less-enlightened times.)

In short, the beginnings of man's physical fears occur at his first awareness of anatomical differences, and the terror that his exposed anatomy could be harmed. This fear of being castrated makes men more anxious than women throughout their entire lives.

This same apprehension also lays the groundwork for a boy's entrance into the Oedipal phase. His desires for Mom become romantic. But the boy's rival is Dad. Bigger and stronger, Dad has the capacity to retaliate. These fears of retaliation stay centralized around the physical source—the penis and testicles—and the dreaded injury remains focused upon castration. These fears then combine with various internalized, parental images to form the superego—the agency of the mind that administers guilt. Chapter Three will elaborate upon the formation of guilt.

The castration fear is on-going, pervasive, and manifests in ways that on the surface may seem unrelated.

For instance, completely unrelated physical injuries stimulate castration anxiety. The actuality of *any* injury translates to a man as I can be injured, therefore, my penis can be damaged.

This correlation, immediate and visceral, often remains unconscious. A man may simply deny injury: "It's only a flesh wound." He may intensely over-react, though the exaggeration is often disguised. Such is the case when a man shrugs off an injury or slight, only to redouble his energies in a counter-phobic way. I.e., a boy fearful of heights may become an airline pilot or a mountain climber.

Or, a man may share his reaction with a woman, instantly transforming her from lover to healing mother. In far more common cases, however, the man under-responds and then becomes depressed— a reaction to symbolic castration.

So the *fear* of castration instigates an eternal quest to protect manhood. And man does this by *proving* the very manhood he seeks to protect.

As is often said in sports, "The best defense is a good offense." Of course, the sporting lament that best belies men's fear of inadequacy states, "Better to be a has been than a never was."

## COMPETENCY

How then, does competency alleviate the fear of castration? A young boy, through his first minor accomplishments and "mastery," undoes his own fear of inadequacy. At the heart of man's psyche, this is experienced as potency vs. impotence, or castration. By achieving small, then larger victories, a developing male not only alleviates fears of impotency, but learns to enjoy the pleasures of success. If the *real* fear is never mastered, a man lives in the defense, becoming the swaggering machismo character who seems to have a "glass jaw."

For many men, this defines the central core of their personas. In *The Streets of Laredo*, Woodrow F. Call finds himself gravely though not mortally wounded. His masculinity, however, never recovers:

"He deeply regretted not doing exactly what Gus McCrae had done: letting the wounds finish him. His wounds had finished him as the man he had been. He clung to a form of life; but a worthless form."

Call provides us with an example of a man so "injured" from age, illness, and decreased prowess, that literal death is preferred.

In such cases, even if life continues, a broken man emerges as other parts of his personality failed to develop in the face of overriding machismo.

So what is healthy competence? In *every* successful act of mastery and drive gratification, defensive and regressive elements also play a part. Even after a full psychoanalysis, men still display macho behavior—asserting dominance and turf (at least now these are unconflicted). This behavior is part of the male mind—imprinted with testosterone before birth—and found in the healthiest of men.

Both men and women have competency needs, but the manifestation comes about differently. Women find validation in adult life by a variety of ways, self-esteem hinging on *many* complicated factors. Men, on the other hand, achieve competence in a more straight-line fashion, often defined by particular moments in time.

Ceremonies such as graduation and awards banquets provide external validation. Internal competence is more personal and represents both direct satisfaction (you can win in your mind and not do anything), as well as undoing castration fears. A big difference does exist however, between true internal competence and narcissistic gratification. So let's talk briefly about the latter, in order to flesh-out the former.

Narcissistic gratification (the feeling that one is more "special" than others and therefore deserves to win) plays an on-going part in men's psychic lives, depending upon each one's individual development. Both pleasuring and delusive, it derives from a primary drive, but with a twist. Though everyone *likes* to win, reinforcing grandiose fantasies can feel euphoric to some men. Winning the office baseball pool can stimulate fantasies of being "special" or "magic." These fantasies are intoxicating, but unrealistic and generally unhelpful in coping with life. Publisher's Clearing House plays on these illusions: "You may already be a winner…"

In real life, "The race is not necessarily to the swift nor the battle to the strong, but you can usually bet on it."—Everett Dirksen.

Careers, hobbies, sports, women—all ways men measure competence. At the core, these activities are merely penis-measuring contests to determine pecking order (*not* an accidental name).

The need to assert dominance, usually for breeding territory, is universal among mammals. Observe domestic dogs when two males meet. After a short posturing session with bared teeth and flared nostrils, one of the males will ceremonially "mount" the other, then peace prevails. Any available female will go to the top dog without further negotiation. If this order does *not* occur, an actual fight will ensue, with the same outcome. Domestic animals only began killing each other when *we* trained them to do so, as it goes against all biological order.

The opening sequence to *Butch Cassidy and the Sundance Kid* provides a nice human example of this same behavior. A card player, not knowing his opponent is The Kid, accuses him of cheating. He stands, prepared to draw—hoping to either back down the accused or kill him, in either case to take the spoils. In the ensuing conversation, he learns the true identity of his opponent and, eyes twitching and voice shaking, says, "I …I …didn't know you were the Sundance Kid when I said you were cheatin'!" He has allowed himself to be mounted and can live, as Butch and Sundance quietly collect the winnings and leave.

The way pecking order is determined varies from culture to culture. In our own it is subtle: "He who dies with the most toys wins," or overt: "We're number one!"

*The Medical Staff parking lot:*

*"Wow," my colleague says, stopping me as I drive into work in my new car. After a fourteen-year struggle with unreliable and often unsafe transportation, I finally could afford a truly safe and new car. Unfortunately, I learned, I'd crossed the imaginary line, buying one step up from the chief of staff!*

*"Nice car," my friend continues, "but I think you just fucked your career."*

*Two years later, I was working at another hospital.*

Recent studies about highway traffic cite "testosterone poisoning" for the confounding stoppages on the freeway. Men assert dominance over one another by speeding up and refusing to let other men cut in, causing the speed-up/slow-down wave rhythms responsible for accident-less traffic jams.

When the engineers designed freeways, they forgot to factor in this aggressive part of men's minds.

More seriously, I treated a patient once who took such cut-offs as a mortal challenge. He grew up in an abusive household, watching his father repeatedly beat his mother and then him. Having matured into a huge man himself, my patient routinely beat up *only* other men and *only* if they needed it. Someone who "needed it" seemed to cross his path about twice weekly. The only redeeming quality about this behavior was that his love for his mother prevented him from beating women.

Typically, a man would pass him in traffic, or some other unforgivable sin. He'd pull in front of the car, slamming on the brakes. When the man stopped, he'd challenge the transgressor's masculinity until a fight could be provoked. His record was hitting a man so hard he landed six feet from the origin of the blow, providing bragging rights at many local bars.

Our brief therapeutic encounter lasted only a few sessions. He eyed me suspiciously and said, "They wouldn't send me to see some *kid* now would they?" I was twenty-eight at the time, and had the distinct impression I was about to fall into the category of someone who needed it. He rose, drew a deep breath, looked me in the eye, left, and never returned. I'm now considered a very cautious driver, *never* needlessly cutting off anyone in Dallas traffic. You must learn to adapt to your environment when new data becomes available!

But of course, the drive remains.

*Sunday morning, Dallas, Texas:*

*Deryl and I gaze at our newly acquired motorcycles.*

*"I've heard these mufflers are just penis extenders," I say in my best clinical voice.*

*"Yeah," he answers with a smile, "and I believe mine are bigger."*

Although this issue plays an enormous role in the psyches of men, it's difficult not to laugh at some of the manifestations of the drive. As in the case of the new cure for penis envy, or how to move up in the pecking order without really trying:

"Dreams Do Come True," a *Dallas Morning News* sports-section ad read. "Penile Enlargement." With a relatively simply surgery, a penis could be made longer and wider. Of course, women overwhelmingly complain much more about technique than size, but men want to measure a true winner. For four to six thousand dollars, you, too, can be hung like a horse.

Curiously, a Dallas urologist criticized the procedure, expressing concern. "The penises I saw in the photos prior to surgery looked about average to me," he said. "And as a urologist, I see a lot of penises." He wondered if many patients needed psychological treatment more than surgical enhancement.

Women grow weary of this issue in a relatively short amount of time. Often I've heard them ask, "Why don't you guys just tattoo the length on your foreheads and avoid all the trouble?"

Like most things in life, however, the struggle is, in and of itself, satisfying and exciting. Every man feels much larger in his own mind and sets out to prove this to the world.

It is wise to remember of course, as the Roman satirist Juvenal put it so well, "If you run out of luck, it doesn't matter how long your penis is."

Internally—where he lives—each man must battle his own fears of incompetence and castration. He does this, in the process growing into maturity, by achieving a sense of mastery and then recalling those events when needed. All men must, to some degree, as Soren Kierkegaard said, "Choose to find your own selfhood."

Every man has defining moments—the imprint of victory and defeat. It may be the day he ran for the game-winning touchdown, passed the CPA exam, or received the key to the executive men's room. Or perhaps, the time he "Made it with the red-haired girl in the Chevrolet" (apologies to Billy Joel). But ask any man, and he can tell you his moments.

"I was not the lion, but it fell to me to give the lion's roar." —Winston Churchill

*Two a.m., cancer ward:*

*"His fevah, doctah. Come," is all the nurse can say in her broken English.*

*I am being beeped in a thousand-bed teaching hospital—a green intern, three months out of medical school. Two a.m., and just over halfway through my thirty-six hour shift. My resident is nowhere to be found.*

*The patient bleeds from all orifices. One hundred and three-point-five degree fever. This man is sick. He needs a doctor! I whisper almost audibly, "I am a doctor. And I'm the only one here."*

*The man survives my shift (a badge of competency for all interns).*

That was one of my moments. Of course, I've had many moments where I've failed, or chosen incorrectly, or simply didn't measure up. But I've often called on experiences such as this one when I needed to bolster my competence and take charge.

All men have moments such as this in their lives and would, by the way, love to tell you about them. Because even after failure, a man can rise above his defeat to once again become the victor. The drive to succeed never dies.

> *"But a man is not made for defeat," he said.*
> *"A man can be destroyed but not defeated.*
> — Hemingway, *The Old Man and The Sea*

Some writers theorize that man's need to be successful is external—imposed from without by society, culture, religion, etc. This is true in the sense that society provides acceptable channels for the river of aggression to flow.

However, if only two men lived in a town, they would both strive to subtly or overtly express dominance over each other. And if only one man lived in the town, he would be driven to master internal fears and anxiety to successfully control his environment.

Or, as Johnny Chapman, Bosque County Constable, said of living in his hardscrabble, rural landscape, "Hell, it wouldn't take much for a man to live in this country. Just a roll of good barbed wire and some bacon." The implication being that a *real* man needs little more than his own resources to survive.

The drive to succeed is internal, centered in the life forces within every cell of the body. The history of mammalian evolution provides a testimonial to this— the most successful organisms survive, conquer, and pass on the genes. The legacy of this drive continues in the psychic forces of *all* behaviors to conquer, dominate, and succeed. A kinder, gentler society may *quell* the drives somewhat, or channel them into creative and productive pursuits, but certainly not extinguish them. A violent, aggressive society simply stokes the fears already in existence.

Clint Eastwood faces down a bad guy to open the movie, *Dirty Harry*. Pistol pointed, he snarls, "You've got to ask yourself, 'do I feel lucky'? Well, do you, punk?" This character found his niche in a smarmy, crime-infested world. But his own aggressive drive *already* surged inside.

In Herman Hesse's novel, *Sidhartha*, we see an example of a man attempting to deny his drives. He practiced to "think, fast, and wait" so as not to be forced into action by instinct. A zealot, he drew awe from those around him for his dedication.

As life progresses, however, our hero's resolve breaks and lo and behold, we find him living with a prostitute, engaging in gluttony, and taking up the profession of a merchant! What happened to our resolute pilgrim?

Unable to learn how to live with and utilize his drives, Sidhartha was at the mercy of his primitive wants when the dam broke and those desires surged through. This is a common Hesse theme as many characters struggle to integrate animal features (Steppenwolf: the wolf of the Stepps) with culture and sophistication. If walled off separately, they never mesh.

To live in *relative* peace, the drives must be owned and directed—a lifelong task.

Poor Sidhartha *did* finally find peace, but only at life's end as a ferry man, with deep yearnings to merge with mother-water. Perhaps an early intervention could have made life much smoother *and* less confusing for him.

As with all drives, we are born aggressive, not made so. Joseph Campbell, after a lifetime of studying the rituals and practices within all cultures said:

"In primitive societies the violence delivered to young men in their teens is prodigious and it is taming them. The young male is a compulsively violent piece of biology and you've got to integrate that."

Our society incorporates male aggressiveness into it in many ways, sports being the best accepted. As NFL coach Mike Ditka said, "Football is really not a contact sport, it's a collision sport. And it's a matter of skill, strength, endurance, and strategy. But I think when it comes down to it, people just like to hit each other."

One way or another, how a culture "integrates that" becomes the sociological issue and is, of course, another book. Our concern centers upon the drives *within* individual men in any society.

Historically, young men have set out on "quests"—rites-of-passage into manhood. King Arthur sent his knights on the quest for the Holy Grail. They searched far and wide for years, looking for that elusive, symbolic *something*. It was a matter of honor.

The Crusades, the Golden Fleece, the key to the executive washroom, full partnership, board certification, my own business—men throughout the generations have gone on quests. These may be spiritual, intellectual, or practical, but are a part of the innate aggressive drive.

A colleague of mine, after finishing his internship, bought a motorcycle and drove to Colorado. He rode to the top of Pike's Peak, drove home, and "sold the damn thing." A quest, you see, can be metaphorical.

Men often spend entire careers searching for the "magic bullet" to cure a disease, or for the meaning of life, or to own the majority share of the stock in their company. All quests are externalizations of man's search for competence and mastery of his drives and conflicts; to explain the internal by way of the external. Even if understood through therapy or analysis, the need to prove oneself will remain. Divert your man from his quest at your own risk! Far better, latch on for the ride. It will most surely be worth it.

Of course, competence (along with all parts of mastery) is not an exclusively male issue. We emphasize the male psyche here as this book concerns understanding men. Women's trek to self-esteem and competence is more varied and difficult, but seeks the same goal—autonomy, with the ability to relate to both women and men.

"Courage is resistance to fear, mastery of fear, not absence of fear," Mark Twain said. And all of us during our quests pull from many sources in times of need.

*Cosmic Caverns, Arkansas:*
*Jill turns four years old next month. Sally, almost*
*six, gleefully skips into the mouth of the cave with her*
*mother, her internal dragons quiescent. For Jill,*
*something is too much. The gaping hole, the darkness,*
*the weird guide? She cannot articulate her fears. I*
*feel her heart beating as I reassure her in the parking*
*lot where I caught her, a safe distance from "the*
*beast." Finally we re-approach the opening with*
*encouragement from Mom and Sis.*

*At the last moment, Jill squeezes my hand tightly.*
*"I be Brave Heart Lion, Daddy." And in we go.*

I am well into mid-life and still find occasion to
call on "Brave Heart Lion" (or his equivalent) to help
me face my fears. You probably do too.

## CASTRATION FEARS AND RELATING TO WOMEN

Men often fear that sexual contact with women
somehow robs them of their masculine powers. As the
poet Robert Frost said in "Home Burial," "A man
must partly give up being a man/With womenfolk...."

And though Frost wrote of the entire relationship
to women, that relationship is, at its core, sexual.

The arena of sports provides a wonderful example
of this fear. One school of thought proclaims that
men's avoidance of women before competition is
merely the adult remnant of "cooties," but the

superstitions proliferated throughout locker rooms well into the '70s. The first male athlete in fact to speak openly on the subject was Dave Waddel, who reported having sexual intercourse with his wife on the morning he broke the world record in the 800 meters, winning the Olympic gold medal.

Teams now debate the "sex vs. no sex" argument, perpetuating the idea that contact with women saps an individual athlete of his prowess (effectively castrating him). After all, Delilah *did* cut off Samson's hair while he wasn't paying attention (sleeping). The premise is defeat-through-victory for the man, as a woman somehow magically removes his manhood through his semen.

Since this is not a physiological phenomenon (ask Mr Waddel), we must look into the minds of men for the origin of the myth. It is buried, once again, in men's fears of engulfment or castration by women, as well as guilt for attaining that which "feels too good."

If boundaries are poor or dependency too great, the merger is a "Tar Baby," where a man can lose himself. Plus, his erection disappears after sex (nobody ever said men were smart on this one), reawakening castration fears, as well as risking retaliation for attaining the forbidden love object. A healthy sense of self and a reality check or two help men with all of these.

This healthy sense of self denotes a person who is comfortable being who he is. Anyone would rather be young than old, rich than poor, strong than weak. But if a man is old, poor, and weak, he can still feel good about himself. Separation, shame, castration, and guilt all evoke fears, but need not remove his ability to regulate self-esteem. This is the goal of psychological health sought by most analysts, and summed up by *Forrest Gump*:

Millie: "Forrest, don't you dream about who you're going to *be* someday?"

Forrest, perplexed: "Won't I be me?"

The *real* issue surrounding sports and sex, however, goes back to men's competitions with each other, and the difficulty in maintaining focus when women are around. A team develops internal dissent when they compete with each other instead of the other tribe (it is forbidden for the Dallas Cowboy Cheerleaders to date Dallas Cowboys). For men to work as a unit, they need singularity of purpose, and the sex drive needs to be sublimated to the common cause.

Team goals can be paramount, but all men maintain the wish to win, to dominate, and to lead. Psychologically, they must prepare for the battle.

Most men have pre-competition rituals that center their minds on the challenge ahead. World Heavyweight Champion John L. Sullivan frequented bars. "I can lick any man in the house!" he would say, each time he entered a bar.

My own pre-race ritual for college swim meets prepared me to override all reality testing (we had two Olympians and fifteen All-Americans on my team alone), *and* all levels of anxiety so that at the moment the gun sounded, I (psychotically) believed I would win the race. This was *absolutely* necessary for peak performance. My eventual finish (I won few college races) did not dampen my enthusiasm *or* my preparation for the next race. Before the big race, big game, big trial, and big deal, all men psyche-up and expect to win.

Again, this is not so terribly different from women, who have their own way of pysching-up. Defeat, however, is dealt with differently by gender. For women the feeling is: "I'm no good." Women feel flawed and defective. Men experience defeat as: "I'm castrated." As Norm Van Brocklin, former coach of the Atlanta Falcons said following a lopsided loss to Miami, "It was a butt-kicking contest, and we supplied the butts."

These feelings must be overcome, however, for the man to strive again. The comeback man of the century, Richard Nixon, said, "The good thing about life is it's ninety-nine rounds." We can assume his psyche-up for each round was effective.

As life-phases alter our aims, our internal needs also change. A teenage boy strives to win in sports and school mainly to garner attention from girls.

This continues throughout a man's life, but is most apparent in adolescence. "And whatever their conscious motives, men seek success to draw women" (*Time* magazine report on "Infidelity").

All males need the feeling of competency and mastery, and must somehow balance that with true merging with women. Young-adults, struggling for autonomy, separate from home. They strive for professional identity while at the same time beginning a new family. Life gets trickier after this.

The thirties comprise a time of consolidation of career choice, as well as parenting skills. Setbacks occur as the vitality of youth is overwhelmed by career frustrations and marital discord, combined with decreasing physical stamina and abilities. The forties challenge a man head-on as career goals are realized (or not) and decreased sexual abilities must be acknowledged and accepted.

The fifties and sixties prepare a man to let go of certain ambitions, only to enjoy the richer substitute of depth relationships and emotional breadth.

Man's highest order of psychic accomplishment is the ability to pass on something of value to the next generation, mainly through mentoring or teaching. Death awaits us all, bringing loss at all levels of psychological function—separation, castration, even punishment. To master our inner fears allows us the opportunity to face death with sense of resolve and dignity. And our moments help us to do this more easily, at any age.

*My driveway, 8:30 a.m., Saturday:*
*Tim passes the ball high and left and I deftly slide away from my defender. With a drop of my left*

*shoulder, I leap slightly away from the bucket, perfectly arching a hook off the glass and through the net. "Game."*

*For an instant, I am kindred spirits with Michael Jordan and Dr. J., certain not even Akeem Olojiwan could have blocked my shot. Heaving and drenched with sweat, I collapse with my middle-aged cohorts in a lawn chair, swilling diet coke (my breakfast). The moment passes. But the rush remains, then is carefully put away to be recalled on demand. Small doses of primitive narcissism can be intoxicating, even in the old men's basketball league.*

Probably an over-forty George Foreman said it best though, before his first fight with Holyfield: "I may be old and I may be fat, but here I is."

We've discussed sports here because showing a man's competency through that arena is clear. Always remember, however, that athletics provide males with the perfect outlet to preen in front of females. So, a man can feel both a sense of mastery, and make a good impression on women at the same time. For the time being anyway, his castration fears are banished.

## COMPETENCY AND RISK
*"Because it was there."*
—Sir Edmund Hillary

Before women's "Running with the Wolves" was acknowledged or socially acceptable, men have "Run with the Bulls." Pamplona, Spain is the site of the ultimate macho, counter-phobic, castration-tempting, male-bonding event. Popularity and overcrowding have now cost the race its charm, but the reasons men run, immortalized by Hemingway in *The Sun Also Rises*, and Michener in *The Drifters* (as well as by countless others) remains the same.

Why *do* men travel halfway around the world to run inches from the horns of wild animals, along with hundreds of complete strangers?

*Counter-phobic* means to do what you fear most with the hope of mastery. As we have seen, the drive for mastery is a generally healthy coping mechanism needed by all men (and women). At its core is the need to undo castration (the risk of real injury) by tempting fate. How many coming-of-age stories have you seen where boys play chicken with trains, cliffs, or cars? Perhaps you witnessed this first hand in high school. Girls usually find these behaviors ludicrous (not to mention terrifying and deadly), but the object is for the male to tempt fate and emerge intact.

Men who run with the bulls, however, report another motivation as well. They feel kindred souls with other men, strangers *but not*, who share their deepest fears. They report a kinship with the wild beast, as they break the aura surrounding the animal by physical closeness and contact. They are at one spiritually with their fears, exhilarated and relieved when the run ends. We will talk about this more in Chapter Four, but the point is that *all* men at some time feel the urge to run.

So what is competency in men? Is it, "The strongest man in the world is he who stands alone," as Dr. Stockman said in Ibsen's *An Enemy of the People*? Or how about that old (and bad) joke that goes: How many real men does it take to change a light bulb? Answer: *None*. Real men aren't afraid of the dark.

Is competency merely healthy aggressive drive gratification and mastery, or is it phallic narcissism to undo castration fears run amok?

Probably both.

Take Gary Cooper in *High Noon*. His new wife, deputy, friends, even his former girlfriend have *all* abandoned him to face alone four murderers (determined to kill him). The prudent, "adaptive" choice would have been to leave (the external forces truly "out of control," and attempting to change his internal perceptions would not be productive at this point). As a therapist, I likewise would have advised him to "get outa town," perhaps reconciling with his estranged wife at a later date.

But "a man's gotta do what a man's gotta do," so when the whistle blows and the clock strikes high noon, all men—at least in their own minds—rise to meet the train.

The bettor's choice would have been that Gary Cooper's fate included death or debilitating injury. Of course, Cooper killed the bad guys, reunited with his wife, and spat in the eye of his betrayers, all in one climactic scene. Life rarely offers this type of definitive resolution. Still, men specifically seek these situations through counter-phobic behaviors, risking injury and even death to prove their manhood. Healthy men do so in a less dangerous or even symbolic way, where relative risk can be minimized.

It is worthy to note in interviewing the test pilots and astronauts for his book, *The Right Stuff*, Thomas Wolf asked why they pushed the aeronautic limits. The answer most often given was, "To impress the other guys." Penis measuring and camaraderie around Rosie's Bar proved to be the top motivators for these men.

As Chuck Yeager asked his engineer after breaking the sound barrier in the X-1, "What next, Ridley?"

Psychological risk-taking is an example of counter-phobic behavior gone out of control. These may include physical or financial risks, or even promiscuity. All are attempts to undo or face down the fears that scare men the most. The only cure is to become consciously aware of the fear and face it directly, decreasing the need for self-destructive behaviors.

# REDEMPTION

*"Bell rang. Ali went back to his corner. The nightmare he'd been awaiting in the ring had finally come to visit him. He was in the ring with a man he could not dominate, who was stronger than him, who was not afraid of him, who was gonna try and knock him out, and who punched harder than Ali could punch, and this man was determined and unstoppable. And Ali had a look on his face I'll never forget. It was the only time I ever saw fear in Ali's eyes.*

*"It was as if he looked into himself and said, all right, this is the moment. This is what you've been waiting for. This is that hour. And do you have the guts..."*

—Norman Mailer, interviewed in *When We Were Kings.*

(Muhammad Ali subsequently knocked out George Foreman for the heavyweight championship of the world in the eighth round after deploying the novel, now famous, "rope-a-dope" strategy moments after this observation was made.)

No man gets through life without falling down.

Failures, injuries, and death are part and parcel of every human being's life experiences. How a man deals with the real or metaphoric castrations determines, to a large measure, his character.

*Six-South, Neurology Service:*
*Up half the night, I briskly examine my new admission. A seventy-eight-year-old man, a farmer of German extraction. He has suffered a stroke and though now stable, his farming days are over.*
*His right arm and leg are completely immobile. His huge right forearm and hand callused from a lifetime of labor lie useless at his side. He studies my face for a moment and then says, "I was much of a man in my day."*
*Startled, I catch his gaze apologetically. Had I somehow offended him?*
*He smiles. "Don't get old, son."*
*I nod and smile in return, saying, "I'll do my best to avoid it, sir." I shake his good hand and he winks as I leave the room.*
*I picture him as he must have been in his prime; his strong arms pitching bales of hay and setting corner posts. It is how he wishes me to think of him. I honor his wishes, and his advice: I don't take my strong and youthful body for granted that day. In time, I will share his fate.*

Although illness and death come to bear on everyone, others are damaged outside of the norm.For those, lifelong struggles to prove competence are common, especially if real or emotional damage occurs severely and early.

A boy who grows up feeling defective or inadequate from real damage (i.e., actual injury), or emotional damage, is set up to seek redemption throughout his life. Physical inadequacies (Napoleon and his height) prime men for over-competitiveness. Belittling or over-stimulation (sexual trauma) can have the same effect—an internal sense of damage for which compensation must be found.

Again, strength can come from failure, no matter the source of the injury. In the television series *Branded*, Chuck Connors is accused of cowardice, and with his sword symbolically broken, is cast out into the wilderness. For the better part of three TV seasons, he wanders the west seeking redemption. Since the network canceled the show while in reruns, we never learn poor Chuck's fate! Ironically, this is true-to-life, as definitive redemption rarely occurs.

But redemption within himself is a *must*. A man, then, must feel complete, whole, and competent within his own mind to survive life's inevitable setbacks. And all men rely on their "moments."

*Mexico City, age twelve:*
*I am unusually nervous before my race—the fifty freestyle in the Texas/Mexico all-star duel meet. My parents haven't come, and I haven't seen my brothers for days. My chief competitor is accompanied by his dad, who is dead-set on "coaching" him to beat me. Our Mexican rival is heavily muscled with hairy*

*armpits (mine are bare) and the hint of a mustache. My stomach rumbles with tourista.*

*We approach the blocks. I feel alone. Panicky. I should win, but feel suddenly rubbery and light headed. I pause for a long moment and take a deep breath. Something stirs deep inside my chest— something ancient but known. I stare at the far end of the pool. It suddenly seems unusually close. I feel calm. And strong.*

*The race itself flies by in a blur. I look back while breathing and catch a fleeting glimpse of my friend's desperate face—the face of defeat. The big Mexican finishes third.*

I swam competitively for ten years after that, lettering in college and competing against those Olympians. Most of my races ended much differently as I "kissed my sister" (apologies to my co-author) *far* more times than I won. But the ability to get centered and focus has stayed with me in many parts of my life. And on days when I feel overwhelmed by outside forces, perhaps even "outcoached," I can focus on the goal. I feel calm. And strong.

Once a man can accomplish the inner feelings of completeness, wholeness, and competency, he can accept loss of status and prowess in old age with wisdom and grace. If not, each passing year becomes a loss, a threat, with bitterness turned into depression.

As the poem from J.R.R. Tolkein's *The Fellowship of the Rings* goes:

> "All that is gold does not glitter,
> Not all those who wander are lost;
> The old that is strong does not wither,
> Deep roots are not reached by the frost.
>
> From the ashes a fire shall be woken,
> A light from the shadows shall spring;
> Renewed shall be blade that was broken
> The crownless again shall be King."

Redemption leads into the next section—Guilt: assuaging the internal dragons to allow victory without remorse. For once a man feels truly competent, he must then face his own guilt for having "won."

## CASE STUDY

*"...money-making has more to do with emotional*
*stability than with intellect."*
—J.P. Marguard

### Paul

A fully tenured professor in a prestigious medical school, Paul was a pediatric surgeon of some renown. He was referred to me for treatment in a secluded unit for impaired physicians—a special group that must search to find objective treatment.

Hard working and proud, Paul excelled in his residency, working one hundred and twenty hours a week while starting a family with his childhood sweetheart. He realized his dream by attaining the rank of professor in his late thirties. Precocious, driven, and competent, the world seemed his.

But something was horribly wrong.

The stresses of training extracted a toll from Paul, both emotionally and financially. He took to drinking heavily on the nights he wasn't working— a much-needed break from such life-and-death work. During his first years of practice, he worked extra to pay off his training debts. His children grew up without him, and his wife became increasingly disenchanted with her white knight.

The alcohol progressed to self-prescribed medication.

"I needed an efficient means to relax my mind quickly," he later explained. The end came one day in surgery. As he proposed to make the incision, his hand shook so noticeably that the anesthesiologist bodily removed Paul from the operating room.

When, I met him, Paul was crushed; his career and marriage in shambles; all he had worked for close to ruins. Paul's lifelong fears of inadequacy and resultant poor self-esteem had found a "cure" in his career successes. However, the cost was that his life lacked any reasonable balance to care for himself as a person, or his family. He suffered from the disease of chemical dependency, but the chemicals themselves merely covered his fear and eventually, his reality.

As Paul deepened his work, his long-standing doubts emerged. The oldest of a working-class family where few had gone to college and none beyond, Paul carried the burden of the family's generations of marginal careers. In doing so, he received tacit if distant approval from his father. He succeeded in school and superficially in life, but always feared he would fail to carry the banner he had been handed, and would return to his modest beginnings in shame.

Years later, I received a card from Paul's wife saying she once again lived with the man she had fallen in love with long before. He had maintained sobriety and through therapy had found the fears driving him so desperately. His career now progressed with less intensity, but more enjoyment.

The family had downsized their lifestyle to decrease their financial pressures and the need to work more. Paul's children knew who he was.

This is a typical story which, unfortunately, does not always or even often end this way. Men generally have an aversion to therapy, equating it with a sign of weakness or loss of self-sufficiency. A trauma usually must puncture the counter-phobic mechanisms. Often the trauma is in the form of divorce, career setbacks, or bankruptcy and even then, women far outnumber men in treatment. Women are more introspective than men anyway, and for a man, "asking directions" is in itself emasculating.

We see in men a need to deny a dependency on others as this threatens their own sense of autonomy and feelings of competence. This intensifies if they must ask for help from another man as this is akin to asking for quarter, which many men won't do, even in the face of literal death.

Paul was fortunate to be open to treatment and survival without having to lose *everything* first. For phallic, swaggering men, this is rarely the expected outcome.

In fact, let's turn for a moment to an extreme example of the macho-man.

## The Bobbits

The Bobbit case captured all of our attention for many months as John Wayne and Lorena squared off in court. It pitted the right of an abused woman to defend herself vs. a punishment for which *no* crime could justify. Jokes and insults flew across kitchen tables, boardrooms, and cocktail parties as the trial ended in an unsatisfactory no-clear-winner draw. Why the public fascination?

Like Nicole Simpson, Lorena Bobbit provided a symbol for battered women and simply women everywhere. Men were larger, stronger, often physically more intimidating, and seen as abusing their personal power to force women's submission to men's territorial possessiveness. Afraid to fight back or flee, Lorena simply endured as women have for centuries, until she could endure no more and injured John Wayne at the heart of his manhood. She cut off his penis.

Curiously, I have treated several patients who have done this to *themselves*. Psychotic with intense sexual drives, they appeased their guilt by removing the instrument at the source—the penis. Unfortunately, this does not assuage guilt, and the surgical technology that saved Mr Bobbit was unavailable to my patients. They travel through life guilt-ridden *and* penis-less.

But the Bobbit story does not end. There is John Wayne, accused of battery with *another* woman. In his plea, John Wayne quoted O.J. Simpson, somewhat sarcastically, saying, "One hundred percent totally *not* guilty."

And we see him yet again, starring in a porno movie—the ultimate macho act—where his penis is displayed among beautiful women and put to the ultimate test, on camera.

The counter-phobic machismo that drives spousal abuse is stimulated, not quelled, by this type of injury. This case caught our attention because it is us: men and women struggling to assert *and* protect ourselves in a world that no longer supplies the rules.

John Wayne Bobbit is an extreme example of the forces at work in the minds of everyman. Counterphobic behavior to undo castration fears is universal, and can be adaptive.

## THE NIGHTMARE OF SNAKES

As a young boy I was terrified of rattlesnakes. This was both a reality (they proliferated throughout my father's ranch), and an externalization of my own inner fears (this volume is limited in scope and space to provide details—whew!).

*Bosque County, Texas:*
*"Gary, don't move!" The desperation in Mike's voice is stark in contrast to the light mood of a moment before. Returning from a dove hunt, we had leaned our guns against the barbed wire further down, and Mike is now straddled over the fence.*

*Dad and Don are already in the cabin, over one hundred yards away.*

*I hear it too, and my heart sinks—the angry buzz of a rattlesnake, close by. Waist-deep grass surrounds us. At eleven and fourteen years of age, we are terror stricken. We don't dare walk to our guns as we can't pinpoint the origin of the sound.*

*"Dad!" we both yell, fighting back panic. The blood drains from Mike's face as we scream louder. Darkness will cloak us in a matter of minutes.*

*My father appears. He locates the rattler not five feet from Mike's foot, and raises my shotgun to shoot. I see the snake, coiled, its triangular head poised to strike, the buzz of its tail vibrating terror into my very soul.*

*With a deafening explosion, the snake blows into three separate pieces, one remaining airborne for a long second. I am numb, then released.*

Four years later, I was shocked to win second place in the science fair for my precise study of the western Diamondback Rattlesnake. I knew intimate details of the habits of rattlesnakes, the likelihood of being bitten, and the chances of survival if you were. My intellectual and cognitive mastery allowed me to walk unafraid through west Texas pastures, but in my worst nightmares and when my deepest fears were stirred the rattle still buzzed.

Castration fears, death, primitive fantasies of being devoured, punishment for my own wicked thoughts; these had all been aroused by the rattlesnake's buzz. My intellectual pursuits had helped, but not until well into my own analysis did I attain relief from the buzzing rattle, where these fears could finally be addressed and quelled.

Of course, as anyone who ventures into the plains of west Texas can tell you, rattlesnakes are dangerous, but the depth of the fear they symbolize comes entirely from us.

*All* behaviors are "direct expression of a drive, a sublimation of a drive or a reaction to it," said Freud. Even now, understanding my snake fears does not cause me to regret one moment of studying these remarkable reptiles, nor *any* of my career decisions. My science project started my interest in biology, which I chose as my college major, eventually leading to medical school and this writing.

I've enjoyed every moment in spite of the original motivators. An adaptive sublimation *can* be a healthy and enjoyable choice.

# SOLUTIONS

Castration fears come to light for most men as a response to career setbacks or loss of physical powers, usually converging during a man's thirties and forties. His ability to respond and adapt will determine the quality of his remaining years.

Stay aware of this, and know with what he is dealing. If he goes to extremes, bring that to his attention, and suggest therapy.

Remember your man's "moments"—those events that stick in *his* mind—to see into his feelings of competency. And your man doesn't have to have been a World Champion (after all, what percentage of us are) for his times of mastery to play an enormous part in his life.

- Support his need to affirm himself and to prove his competency. Being with you actually is part of this.

- Let him know if this need interferes in a realistic way with connecting to you. His need to prove himself shouldn't mean neglecting you.

- Don't underestimate the importance of his career success to his self-esteem.

- Encourage him to keep up physical activities he enjoys.

- If he gets slammed to the mat, give him time to recover.

## CHECKLIST
## UNHEALTHY MASTERY ISSUES:

1). Does your man seem so driven to succeed that he lets other parts of his life slide, i.e., you? Your children? All men need a balance.

2). Must he always one-up other men? *Constantly* talk about his souped-up car, engine, etc., and how his is better than others? How much he paid for something, how much money he makes?

3). Does he constantly speak of his conquests with women? Or of how women "come on" to him?

4). Is he a macho-man? Intent on proving his manhood?

5). Has he suddenly taken up skydiving, bungee jumping, or another high-risk activity?

6). Must he always win and best others, even you?

7). Is he angry and irritable when he suffers an apparently minor setback?

# CHECKLIST
# HEALTHY MASTERY:

1). Is he able to reasonably relate to you his moments? Are these sources of pride rather than obsession?

2). Can he respond to defeat gracefully (even if he truly wants to win)?

3). Can he accept constructive criticism without becoming defensive or angry?

4). Can he accept advice from other men?

5). Is he proud to be a man, while not needing to constantly reinforce his manhood?

6). Is he able to back down in the face of insurmountable odds? I.e., adapt and choose another course of action?

7). Can he face minor setbacks in stride, taking a reasonable amount of time to lick his wounds and regroup before diving back into the fray?

## QUESTIONS AND ANSWERS

1). Question: My boyfriend always leaves my toilet seat up in *my* bathroom. I've fallen in a few times unexpectedly, and he doesn't seem to care. What gives?

Answer: Other than the overt turf battle (who's in charge), your boyfriend is displaying the number-one complaint in our phallocentric culture—the need for the penis to predominate. For some men, a down seat reinforces that certain people are "penis-less," which is threatening. Reclaim your turf, put the seat down, and send him to his therapist if this escalates into other forms of domination.

2). Question: My husband seems obsessed with his career. He spends his waking hours trying to get ahead or outdo his competition. I enjoy the money and other things that success brings, but I miss *him*. What do I do?

Answer: Men's careers often take on the metaphorical role of proving oneself. Part of this is healthy —an appropriate expression of the aggressive drive— but *can* be destructive if the need to "undo" internal damage (castration) is too strong. Remind your husband who you married (him, not an obsessed CEO). If unsuccessful, insist on him reevaluating his priorities—spouse and family should *always* be number one.

3). Question: Some guy at work always gets my boyfriend's goat. I hear about it *constantly*. I try to be supportive, but the whole thing seems silly—the other guy is just a jerk anyway.

Answer: Your boyfriend is engaged in an old-fashioned "pissing contest"—whose is bigger. There may be *real* issues at stake (i.e., who gets promoted), but likely as not, this has to do with dominance. A good friend points out reality while remaining supportive but eventually sets limits— you didn't go out with him to help plot revenge.

4). Question: My boyfriend pulled a muscle playing tennis and now mopes about constantly. I'm very nurturing, but this injury is no big deal. When do I tell him to make his own soup?

Answer: The symbolic meaning of this injury outweighs any real damage. Again, nurturing can be fun up to a point, but don't infantilize. Tell him you love him *even though* he's damaged—this may go a long way after he's recovered.

5). Question: After being fired, my husband's like a different man. He's depressed to the point of rarely getting off the couch and isn't making his best effort at looking for work. I'm really concerned.

Answer: Clinical depression may be triggered by loss or symbolic damage. By feeling unmanly, your husband appears to be spiraling down into despair.

Insist on treatment—depression is overwhelmingly treatable with the right doctor.

6). Question: My husband talks about sex all the time—dirty jokes, vulgar references—but never seems to actually want to participate. What gives?

Answer: Your husband is using counterphobic, adolescent-like coping mechanisms to defend against performance fears. Calmly state your concerns, but be patient! You may have to discuss this with him many times before he owns up to the behavior. Reassure him, but the fear may be so deep-seated that outside help should be sought.

7). Question: My husband rarely wants sex. How do I tell if this is due to castration fear or low sex drive?

Answer: The most important factor is *change* in his sex drive. If he's never been very active, this may be constitutional or a long-standing inhibition. If his sex drive drops (or rises) around specific conflicts, castration anxiety or depression are the likely culprits.

8). Question: How can I tell if his wanting to start a new activity is just excitement, or is counterphobic? Sometimes the line seems fuzzy.

Answer: A genuine interest in a new activity will be deeply enjoyed and consistent over time. Counterphobic behavior is usually short lived or feels defensive at the time. If the goal of the activity is to reaffirm his manhood, it's counter-phobic.

9). Question: My boyfriend works on his car all of the time. Is this obsessive/compulsive behavior to defend against his attachment to me, or the sublimation of castration fears to prove he's the biggest?

Answer: It's probably both. As long as he uses the car to take you someplace nice on Saturday night, don't complain. Men's obsessive/compulsive traits are useful if they don't get in the way.

10). Question: If he has an affair to prove his manhood, will that behavior continue? Is there anything I can do?

Answer: An affair usually reaffirms a man's sense of being desirable and manly. Unless the underlying causes are addressed, it will likely recur. You can help by setting firm limits with zero tolerance of future behavior. Be available to talk with him if the feelings driving the need for an affair emerge.

11). Question: How much risk taking is *too* much? Don't all men need to take risks now and then to prove they "still have it"?

Answer: Men have a need to prove it to themselves every day. A healthy sense of mastery improves self-esteem and assures competency (this is the same for both sexes). Risk taking that involves real danger (physical, emotional, financial) is inherently self-destructive and actually *undermines* self-esteem. Learn to tell the difference.

12). Question: My husband was belittled in childhood by his father, and though he has undergone therapy for this, he still shows signs of the abuse. Will this ever go away?

Answer: Often a man with this background will make use of the lessons of therapy long after termination and "cure" into a much stronger identity. Be patient.

13). Question: My boyfriend has a bad temper. He's only pushed me once or twice. But will this escalate into violence? I try to praise his manliness as much as possible.

Answer: You can have **ZERO** tolerance of physical violence. Men are generally bigger and better fighters and allowing violence puts you inherently "one down." The best relationships are between equal partners. Praising him to bolster self-esteem that is damaged enough to push a woman will not be effective.

14). Question: My husband was passed over for a much-coveted promotion. Though he has more seniority—fifteen years with the company—the position was awarded to a much younger man. Devastated, my husband has shown little interest in *anything* since this happened. I know it hit his manhood hard, but what can I do?

Answer: Allow him time to feel the sting and grieve the loss. He must, however, in reasonable time "pull his dick out of the dirt" and face up to what life still has to offer. Be initially supportive, then encouraging, and finally insist that he get off the sidelines and back into the game.

## Chapter Three
# The Third Key:
# Pure and Simply Guilt

*"Now I am become Death, the destroyer of worlds."*
—Frank Oppenheimer, as he watched the first atomic
bomb explosion during the Trinity Project, recalling
Vishnu's words from *The Bhagavad Gita.*

## THE CONSCIENCE

Men are riddled with guilt. Most women find this statement preposterous. But were it not for guilt and man's need to adhere to internal standards, we would live in a far more violent and dangerous world. Fear, shame, and depression cannot begin to impact a man in the way in which does guilt.

*"I've a very pessimistic view of life ...I feel that life is divided up into the horrible and the miserable ...The horrible would be like, uh, I don't know, terminal cases, you know, and blind people, crippled ...And the miserable is everyone else. That's all. So, when you go through life, you should be grateful that you're miserable."*
—Alvy Singer (Woody Allen) in *Annie Hall*

Can someone give this man a referral? This is the essence of guilt-laden neurosis, and is, fortunately, quite treatable.

As discussed in Chapter One, the "good" and "bad" mothers have fused into one whole in the boy's mind by ages three to four. This evokes a complete image of mother within. Then, with the Oedipal struggle, the fear of retaliation (castration) from father intensifies. Guilt over sexual desires for Mom and the wish to banish Dad, walks hand-in-hand with that fear.

A healthy boy enters the Oedipal Phase with an internal ability to fuse objects. He experiences the drive to win what he wants as an integral part of himself. He then becomes aware that his new love for Mommy has a new twist: perhaps *we* could have what she has with Dad. But Dad is bigger, and I've seen him angry. This fear is internalized in the superego, commonly known as our conscience—the regulator of guilt.

Also around the ages of five to six, the parental commands of "No," and "Better not do that," become internalized as the superego develops, and *true* guilt emerges.

True guilt goes beyond the fear of our parents and the loss of their love, beyond retaliatory fears of father. True guilt implies fear of our *own* conscience—both its wrath and the loss of its love. In other words, the condemnation of the parent is internalized. And the boy then "owns" this.

Without such guilt, a man would have no conscience. I have often related human drives with those of primates, and the very quality of guilt is what separates us from them. As Martin Buber says, "Man is the being capable of becoming guilty and is capable of illuminating his guilt."

Guilt shapes us all. But it is a double-edged sword, especially for men. To avoid the fates of castration or oblivion (being "banished" by father), guilt keeps men from pushing too far and "winning" too much. It provides the internal answer to anarchy.

We all know the old saying, "Be careful what you wish for—you just might get it." In psychoanalytic terms, this is a truism. What often limits talented people is not external constraints, but the internal mechanism of guilt—winning comes at too high a cost.

The story that most transfixed guilt in Freud's (and now everyone's) mind is the Greek tragedy of Sophocles, *Oedipus Rex*. In this tale, an aggressive king *inadvertently* kills his father and makes love with his mother. Upon learning of his transgressions, he "castrates" himself by gouging out his own eyes. He then spends his remaining days under the care of his two daughters.

Of course, the need for this severe punishment comes from the fact that Oedipus, being a psychologically intact male, had secretly wished to do this as a boy.

If you *unwittingly* hurt someone, you feel loss and some shame for being thoughtless. It passes relatively soon. If you instead accidentally (or not) do something you *wanted* to do but have forbidden yourself from doing, you feel guilty.

King Oedipus was endowed with a huge aggressive drive, which required an "equal but opposite" reaction by his superego, resulting in tremendous, unconscious guilt. This guilt was triggered when he got what he wished for.

All blood and lust you say? And what of loving and caring—the loss of all possibility of "reuniting" with his family of origin and having a healthy adult/child relationship? Very true, and a real loss. But this pales when compared to the power of unbridled guilt. You don't poke out your eyes because you and your parents can't be friends.

In Freud's classic case of "Little Hans," a boy exhibiting exaggerated guilt and self-abasement is presented for treatment. As therapy progresses, Hans reveals the wish for his father to "go away" so that he may have Mother all to himself. But he also loves Father, and would miss him and truly wishes that Dad, too, could stay around.

In time, Hans gives up his "special" wishes for Mother, with some sadness. But he finds comfort through keeping her in another (pre-Oedipal) way, not to mention saving ol' Dad from exile. The family romance is safely resolved, and little Hans, due to effective early intervention, is symptom free, going on to marriage and a successful, creative career. This good outcome resulted from "talk" therapy, allowing Hans to integrate his drives while minimizing guilt and real danger.

A modern tale of harsh, primitive superego function can be seen in the *Star Wars* films. Fatherless Luke Skywalker is caught in a violent struggle with an "evil" father (Darth Vader—Dark Father). Two guiding, "good" fathers (Ben Kenobi and Yoda) help Luke. The romantic love object (Princess Leia) is present but this aim is vague. Primarily, the story concerns aggression, beginning with unfused, early objects.

It is the vindictive, murderous, "past" object (Vader) who plagues poor Luke and who must, in the end, be won over. Luke struggles through three feature films, killing countless bad guys, until in the final scene, all—Luke, Obi-Wan Kenobi, Yoda, Darth Vader, Leia, Chewbacca, and Hans Solo—are reunited (fused) into one symbolic psyche.

If the good and bad objects are split or defective prior to the Oedipal Phase, this type of sequence occurs. It may take three feature films (or one analysis) to resolve. Hopefully, a relationship with a woman is next for Luke.

In Chapter Two, we discussed the quests upon which men embark, and that the reasons for these quests are many. Joseph Campbell described the hero's journey not so much as a courageous act, but as a life lived in discovery. He said, "Luke Skywalker was never more rational than when he found *within* himself the resources of character to meet his destiny." (Italics mine.)

In real life, the Oedipal struggle is likely to play out in more subtle ways. As this part of development is similar in both boys and girls (to opposite-gender parents), one example illustrates the dynamics.

I once sat on the edge of a pond with my oldest daughter, Sally, then four, who told me a tale about our webbed-footed friends:

*A duckling swims close to a mallard drake, the hen is not in sight.*

*"Maybe the mommy's gone," Sally offers, beaming. "And the baby gets to go live with the daddy at the office."*

*I assure her the mommy will return soon and all will live together. Disappointed, then puzzled, and finally, calm, Sally walks with me hand-in-hand back to the house.*

## GUILT, AGGRESSION AND SOCIETY

Society will not, indeed *cannot,* save us from ourselves. Not our laws, our machines, not even our science can overcome aggressive drives. As Thomas Hobbes said, "Laws are designed to protect man from his own brutish nature." In essence, these merely provide tools with which we can work. This does not deny the effects of the outer world, but rather emphasizes that none of these can master man. His own "inner" world must be intact before he submits to the laws of society.

Rousseau, the eighteenth-century French philosopher, felt that man in his natural state is good. The quest for private property brings out the brute. The anthropologist Richard Leakey, in *Origins*, talked at length about modern huntergatherer tribes being relatively free of violence or rape, pointing blame for these ills on urbanization. The poet Robert Bly, in *Iron John*, takes a similar stance by stating that the violence in our inner cities is cultural—caused by the lack of male role models to guide young men.

All of these explanations are correct. But there is more to the story.

The drive to kill exists in every cell of our bodies, and its psychic expression lies in aggression. The goal of this drive is to assert dominance and breeding territory. In nature, all confrontations between rival males *end* when one shows a decisive edge. The group (herd, tribe, clan, etc.) cannot afford to lose valuable members.

This gives way in people when the internal control mechanism is damaged (the superego, malformed), allowing the wish to kill to emerge unchecked, *or* when the external circumstances are so severe as to threaten survival. Even a rabbit can be a formidable fighter when cornered.

The old (and sexist) saying is that "all starving men eat in the same way." We can all be reduced under stress to the killers who lurk within. But you cannot stimulate *nothing* and have aggression result. The aggression existed in the first place.

And as Joseph Campbell put it, "...the hero's journey ...is not to deny reason. To the contrary, by overcoming the dark passions, the hero symbolizes our ability to control the irrational savage within us."

Robinson Crusoe, alone on the island, aggressively fought to survive, prepared to battle Friday to the death if need be. Crusoe, of course, a man of strong conscience (as well as good powers of intuition and persuasion) converted Friday into a companion—the *adaptive* choice for both partners. But our English gentleman would have quickly killed Friday, "if all else failed."

Joseph Conrad's *Heart of Darkness* takes us further, as the narrator tells Kurtz's tale. "The Inner Station was the farthest point of navigation and the culminating point of my experience."

And so it is within us all.

Kurtz, drawn into the darkness, has lost his humanity: "The wilderness echoed loudly within him because he was hollow at the core." A good description of a faulty and malfunctioning superego. Kurtz's individual, spiritual journey ends with his words, "The horror!"

Conrad paints a good picture of how aggressive drives can run amok when the superego fails to balance them.

But the drives themselves are both necessary and useful. We enter the world screaming and fighting. The Apgar score is based on "vigor" or fight. The passive, or those lacking the will to live quickly fade. In cancer patients, people who fall outside of the predicted survival curve are the ones with a strong will to live on the upside, and those who give up on the down.

A boy born in the inner city has within him an innate aggressive drive. If he has no father, he has no one to identify with, as Bly said. But also, he has no one to fear in order to develop superego function.

What happens when the superego has not developed? What *horror!* did Kurtz speak of? What function kicks in when no conscience exists?

Primitive narcissism takes over.

Primitive narcissism arises from infancy and remains in some form throughout life. The *degree* to which it influences the psyche is the key. It serves a psychotic function that can be used defensively or in a healthy way to deal with a conflict—a *little* grandiosity is healthy (it helped me when competing against Olympians). "Ah, but a man's reach should exceed his grasp/Or what's a heaven for?" —Robert Browning. The trick is to remain grounded in reality to avoid the crash.

Primitive narcissism is fueled by the sexual and aggressive drives. Without an intact conscience, it can run dangerously amok. This is where guilt can serve as society's *and* an individual's greatest ally.

Often, the lines between law and order and the "right thing" become blurred.

*Sierra Madre Mountains, North of San Luis Potosi, Mexico:*

*The train pushes up into the mountains, leaving the prairie lands far behind. At the last stop, we notice "Federales" have boarded. Their shiny helmets and machine guns gleam, striking and ominous, in stark contrast to the commonly dressed Mexicans who dominate the rest of the train.*

*In broken English the conductor explains, "The banditos in these mountains are ruthless—they have no remorse."*

*We stare at the intimidating soldiers. Les, one of my medical school traveling buddies, says under his breath, "Okay, so who protects us from them?"*

*I go to bed that night two hundred pesos ahead in our progressive poker game, carefully placing my wallet under my arm. We awake to anguished voices —the banditos came anyway.*

*Many passengers were relieved of their dinero in spite of our protective "Federales." But the thieves did show remorse—each victim finds both visa and passport tucked carefully under his pillow, not unlike the tooth fairy.*

*"They wanted their money," the conductor explains, "not their souls."*

*Honor still exists among thieves, whose need for money is tempered by their ability to experience remorse.*

With superego intact, the male functions in a healthy manner. The degree of guilt is directly proportional to the degree of lustful and aggressive drives. By definition, you need strong guilt to temper a strong drive.

In a psychotic state, primary narcissism overtakes the superego *and* reality testing (a man may truly believe he's Napoleon). But primary narcissism also comes into play whenever healthier functions fail. This is especially true when Oedipal issues are unresolved or not addressed (i.e., no dad), which leaves a healthy superego overruled by grandiosity.

Often, powerful external forces are needed to combat grandiose behavior. Such as jail. Even there, many maintain an arrogant, defiant stance.

Injury occurs when this narcissism is internally punctured, and a person must come face to face with what he is defending against. A man will most likely deny realistic physical limitations or castration fears with the belief that he is "great" (great athlete, lover, etc.). When reality intervenes (i.e., shot down by a woman), the underlying fear bursts through, with powerful impact. He will experience overwhelming feelings of inadequacy or even self hate. Self-destructive behavior may follow.

Combine primitive narcissism with the violence and drugs around the ghetto, and many youth become "Superfly"—ten feet tall and bulletproof. Criminals (pimps, drug dealers, thieves) ascend to the top of the socio-economic ladder, giving this lifestyle its social sanction. This sets the stage for the "wilding" gangs to emerge.

These baddest-of-the-bad boys are often shocked when injured or caught. Of course, it feels better to fantasize about being Superfly than to accept a fate of poverty and limited hope for success. I have treated psychotic patients who were unwilling to give up their delusions. These delusions felt too good when compared to reality.

In truth, the gang members lack role models and male teachers, but more importantly, they lack an internal sense that an act is wrong or shameful.

I've never met a patient with *no* guilt, but often see young men with defective internal inhibitors, over-run with primitive narcissism.

One such patient came from a well-to-do family with a weak and ineffectual father, and an over-gratifying mother. He became involved with crime and drugs at an early age, and was diagnosed as a pure sociopath—virtually *no* evidence of guilt.

This man transferred from another psychiatric hospital where he had attacked his psychiatrist with a two-by-four, and put two aides in the hospital. He arrived in a body cast (the airlines forbade shackles).

I worked with him for many months. He was prone to primitive rages and had little interest in others' feelings. Interestingly, he made a reasonable connection with me. I never felt scared.

One day he ran away. Several months later he stole a gun and took a motorist hostage with the intent to kill him. At the last minute, our former patient released the driver and turned the gun on himself.

Guilt was there with him, just not always in evidence. Or, perhaps, as one member of our staff said thoughtfully, our treatment was successful after all.

This wish to kill, the urge to rape, and primitive guilt are in every man. How they are shaped and sublimated determines his character.

Joseph Campbell often lamented our failure "to admit within ourselves the carnivorous lecherous fever" that is endemic to human nature. However, he also said, "It is not society that is to guide and save the creative hero, but precisely the reverse."

## HEALTHY VS UNHEALTHY GUILT

I doubt the men around you are either psychotic or sociopathic (more on these in Chapter Six), but the extremes help in our general understanding of guilt and the superego. So what about help for the more "normal" man?

A major function of psychoanalysis or depth therapy is first to understand the formation of an individual's guilt. Guilt can then be re-formed to allow for greater satisfaction in life, while the man still lives within society's bounds. To accomplish this, you must "bring your parents into the room," as the superego is formed by internalizing *their* condemnations.

Guilt is almost completely unconscious. That is, until a standard is transgressed (King Oedipus), or conscious insight is attained.

The latency years (ages six to eleven) are largely composed of re-working internal standards through rules and conditions. This allows boys to connect with other boys and to vent aggressive behaviors. While no one gets killed or even driven off, collective internal standards set "the rules."

Rules are our legacy from latency. Watch groups of seven-year-old boys "play" a game and you'll see that easily one-third of the energy goes into establishing the rules.

A friend's ten-year-old son formed a club in his neighborhood. After clearing a spot outside for tables and chairs, the children sat for days, specifically delineating the rules of their club—an organization which ultimately did *nothing* but have rules!

This also provides a good argument for sandlot as opposed to organized sports (where all rules are already set). Boys need this rule-setting behavior. As

Robert Bly says, rules are "the precepts that help us control our madness."

Boys who must set their own rules for behavior or games develop a working model of fairness and empathic "fair play," as opposed to rigid external standards imposed from outside. This flexibility— reworking superego standards to adjust to the given situation—is adaptive for the individual's psychic functioning *and* integration into the group (eventually society).

This constraint of rules ensures fair play, but really protects boys from the emergence of primitive aggressions with fears of injury or guilt. Woe be unto the one who wins but breaks the rules!

Kids' (or adults') level of functioning can be observed in many ways. One example is the attachment a boy has to comic-book characters. Superman is a narcissistic, magical being. In fact, kryptonite is needed just to make the stories interesting. The Flash is also superhuman and magical.

Captain America, Batman, and the like are higher-functioning characters. They need no superhuman powers, just a working knowledge of their strengths and limitations. Without magic, they maximize their own potential.

In adult life, this translates into a man's fascination with invulnerable characters (James Bond never dies), as opposed to real people who may win or lose based on persistence, intelligence, and more human vulnerabilities and strengths.

Clint Eastwood in the spaghetti westerns showed no fear and always prevailed, regardless of the odds. On the other hand, Gary Cooper in *High Noon* struggled with fear, guilt, and *real* danger of injury (he bleeds when cut), all of which is left unresolved until the movie's final scene.

So, what does all this mean in terms of the man in one's life now, and how can it help you choose wisely?

A study published by Vaillant at Harvard can help us. This fifty-year study followed Harvard male sophomores through life. The men who used healthier coping styles were happier, physically healthier, had better marriages, more successful careers, and lived longer than those who employed more primitive coping styles. The most successful (and happiest) men had surpassed their fathers in socio-economic station. They navigated the minefield of the Oedipus, avoided guilt, and allowed for the pleasure of an enjoyable life. But how did they do this?

Healthier styles include sublimation (diverting the drive), anticipation, altruism, and humor.

Sublimation can be as simple as hitting a golf ball instead of your boss, or as complex as planning an independent business. You divert the drive to allow gratification without evoking guilt, or pissing off too many people.

Anticipation is the opposite of poor impulse control—which is easy to spot. To anticipate is to be able to project yourself into a situation and try out solutions in your *mind* first. The skiing and golf cybernetics are based on this. Impulse-driven individuals, on the other hand, experience rather miserable existences. They live at the mercy of their drives.

Every woman I've ever treated wants a man with a sense of humor, not sarcastic nor vindictive, but as an expression of experiencing genuine joy in living.

Altruism is the capacity to put the needs of others temporarily ahead of your own (although *not* in the sense of tithing forty percent to someone). True altruism is close to generativity—the passing on of something of value to others—and is ultimately based on love. There is a fine line between altruism and masochism, but it can be discerned. Masochism is "pleasure in pain," but often is simply volunteering for pain to avoid greater punishments later.

The primitive or sick mechanisms that predict an unhappy, unsuccessful life are *projection* (I'm unhappy because you do x), *denial* (I didn't do it), and *splitting* (the unfused Darth Vader/Ben Kenobi from *Star Wars*).

These primitive defenses develop during the first years of life, and all humans use them to deal with internal conflicts and the external world. Under ideal circumstances, a child masters the denial conflicts consciously and completely, and goes on to more mature coping mechanisms.

Therapy and analysis work in reverse, going backward into the unconscious conflicts, helping the individual resolve them and utilize healthier, more adaptable coping skills to deal with the intense feelings involved.

Of course, someone who relies on primitive defenses is the *least* likely to tolerate the closeness of therapy, and experiences observations as intrusions. This type of work proceeds slowly, with a great deal of time spent establishing a trusting relationship on the front end.

In treatment, early fears of abandonment, shame, or castration are re-exposed with the therapist, and adult coping skills can be used. As an individual is freed-up from repressed conflicts, he can then utilize more mature defenses.

Obviously, the healthier styles work better, so why doesn't everyone use them? Unfortunately, you cannot simply advise someone to use more anticipation, sublimation, and humor, as the conflicts *driving* the more primitive mechanisms have not been addressed. The healthier styles follow conflict resolution.

Men and women both regress under stress to more primitive coping styles. Any of us can become more childlike under the influence of overwhelming stress. Men tend to be generally more rigid than women, and when the rigidity breaks, predictable outbursts appear. Unfortunately for women, the *most* stressful, ongoing issue in most men's lives is the relationship with a woman.

Women complain that men are cold, distant, and dogmatic when pushed, that they become rage-full and blaming, owning little responsibility for their current problems. After the incident, their "other" quickly seals over the rage and emotions, often denying the episode even took place. This drives most women batty. "Why won't he *talk* to me?" they ask.

If this is set in stone, or even routine, consider the "get out" option. If it is rare or nonexistent, consider yourself fortunate. For the most part this behavior is infrequent (though still maddening). Just know that regardless of his denial, he is nonetheless dramatically affected by it.

One must find courage to face the beast within.

## NEUROTIC GUILT

All of us are neurotic. At least, we *hope* we are. Sound odd?

Otto Kernberg, the contemporary Freudian analyst and theoretician, describes *only* three personality types. Psychotic, borderline, and neurotic. Chapter Six will discuss the first two more fully. Just hope your man is neurotic, which spans a wide spectrum.

Neurotic guilt is the inhibitor we all feel when we "win too much," i.e., become more successful than we feel we should. Our avoidance of this guilt is woven into our characters. At the healthier end of the spectrum, we find "conflict free" values. This is always a relative term, as any value arises out of one's own experiences and conflicts.

The degree of guilt is determined by the strength of one's drive, combined with the administrative function of the superego. How flexible and adaptable to insight our superego is (or becomes) to a large extent determines our conflict and enjoyment of adult life. Since most people reading this book will rarely go without a meal or a warm place to sleep, "happiness" is more determined by how we come to terms with our internal demons, and, how we regulate guilt.

*"...I am southern made and southern broken,*
*Lord, but I beseech you to let me keep what I have.*
*Lord, I am a teacher and a coach. That is all*
*and it is enough."*
—Tom Wingo, *The Prince of Tides*, by Pat
Conroy

The pendulum swings widely. Someone with little guilt or concern about their impact on others behaves sociopathically. We tend to call them "assholes" or "jerks." This generally results in some social consequences (not always!). On the healthier end lies the person who doesn't take advantage of others because he would *like* himself less, not necessarily out of fear or guilt.

We see this both in individuals, and in groups as well.

*Taos, New Mexico, 1974:*

*The old Indian sits quietly at a table against the wall, as my colleagues and I talk about the "dig." Anthropology students, we are excavating a burial site, circa 1100, out at the old Pueblo ruins. Excitedly, we review our find—a man, age thirty, over six feet tall, a remarkable specimen and virtually intact. We have learned a great deal about the diet, culture, and habits of these people from this discovery.*

*The old man rises and turns to us before he walks to the door. "You have no right," he says. "These are my ancestors. Their spirits should rest in peace." Before we can respond, he is gone.*

There are cemeteries in London, Berlin, Prague, and Paris with gravesites much older than our site; no one would consider disturbing those. It's been twenty-five years, but his words haunt me still because he was correct. We had no right.

We face guilt in life every day. Common are the myriad of behaviors (giving at the collection plate, stopping at stop signs on deserted intersections, paying the toll when the gate is unattended) that we engage in to assuage or curtail guilt.

Most commonly in my practice, the experience of guilt is seen in individuals not living up to their potential in either career or relationships. Only so much success or pleasure is allowed before self-sabotage sets in. Careful, painful exploration and reliving through therapy can relieve someone of this plight. A full psychoanalysis invariably centers around reliving the formation of the superego, with the analyst playing the original parental roles. The goal is to move into *relatively* unconflicted values, and to provide more internal flexibility of choice. I.e., it expands one's life, opening to more choices while remaining within the parameters of one's values.

A simple-sounding task that may take a great deal of work to accomplish.

Due to the intense fear of castration, superego function is extreme and hopefully, *sharply* defined. The superego is then reworked during the rulesdominated latency period, and throughout adolescence and young adulthood. Significant parental figures (coaches, teachers, mentors) can offer opportunities for fine-tuning the template, but a complete retooling requires therapy or analysis.

## SPIRITUALITY AND THE NEW MAN

The Christian Men's Movement is currently gathering steam in the form of The Godly Man— The Promise Keeper. Akin to the wildman, these men proclaim to keep in touch with their deepest masculine urges while maintaining spirituality and giving leadership to their families and communities. "Safe Sex" is easy, they say, it's called marriage.

This movement catches many men who could not identify with previous men's movements—they would not chant naked with other men while beating their tom-toms. It also reaffirms something many men feel they have lost: leadership within their own families.

While the women's movement has brought equity (according to a CNN factoid, forty percent of working women earn *more* than their spouses), it has left many men uncertain of their roles as husbands, fathers, and community leaders. Of course, the real answer to these issues resides within each man's head. From Fred Flintstone to yours truly, the changing social or economic times isn't responsible for how we feel about ourselves.

However, the Godly Men's Movement attempts to address spirituality in a way others have not—a rigid rules-oriented way, rather than a Buddhist, "at oneness" way.

Each person has a spiritual side to his/her psyche. It can be arguably said to stem from our early life experiences, or, from a Jungian view, our mystical connections with each other. Fundamentalists feel it is our connection to *the* God.

All cultures throughout history have shared this debate, which won't be resolved here. What remains undeniable is the existence of the mystical within all of us.

A man's spiritual side can be an extremely healthy part of his life. It can help him to avoid transgressions that would provoke guilt or social condemnation. It can help him connect in a primitive, yet safe way with other men and women. It can shape his values to improve his life, his marriage, and his parenting. But, as with anything else in a person's mind, it can also serve to avoid conflicts and rationalize self-serving behavior.

Regression into spiritualism, closely akin to aestheticism, is a powerful defense that can be used to avoid conflicts inherent to living. A "closeness to God" can be a way of reliving the longing to be close to Mom *after* an attempt to avoid the anxiety of appropriate aggression in the world.

Conversely, through "forgiveness of sin" (available in *all* religions) most acts of selfishness and brutality can be absolved or even justified. Remember, the Crusades were fought by Godly Men. But the Moslem children's stories tell of brave farmers repelling the invasions of beastly murderers wearing red crosses. History is replete with examples of wanton aggression justified by someone's religion.

As Joseph Campbell said:

"Instead of clearing his own heart the zealot tries to clear the world. The laws of the City of God are applied only to his in-group (tribe, church, nation, class, or what not) while the fire of a perpetual holy war is hurled (and with good conscience, and indeed a sense of pious service) against whatever uncircumcised, barbarian, heathen, 'native' or alien people happens to occupy the position of neighbor."

So what *is* the healthy role of spirituality in each man's life? Obviously, our mystical sides must be accepted and understood at a conscious level, with their defensive functions clearly elucidated. Spirituality must be in balance with the other forces of love, hate, and aggression; one force cannot *replace* another. God's love doesn't make us less aggressive, but can make us less violent. The goal of analysis, and life, is to understand, accept, and live fully. To do this, the Godly Man, the Wild Man, and the Modern Man must become one within the mind of each *individual* man.

And a little humor never hurt:

"I'd like to thank all of you for making the new album a success. I promise to spend your money foolishly." —Jimmy Buffett, following a long description of his lifelong struggle to overcome "Catholic Guilt."

So a man needs to redeem himself *for* himself, to assuage his own internal demons, to make peace inside. Not winning or losing, it truly is how he plays the game that matters most within the psyche.

In 1994, after knocking out Morer to win the heavyweight title, George Foreman said thoughtfully, "I'm thankful not that I won, but that I had the opportunity."

In essence all any man wants is the *opportunity* to win. That is his chance for redemption.

# CASE STUDY

*"Nothing is as difficult to bear as a series*
*of good days."*
—Goethe.

## Ron

Ron was referred to me when he moved to Dallas from out of state. Depressed for some time, he had been in therapy since the breakup of his marriage two years before. Ron had experienced this as a stinging rejection of himself as a person, confirming his oldest fear that he was not lovable. As our therapy progressed, other aspects of his development came to light.

The second of three children, Ron had an exceptionally high energy level as a child. His parents often admonished him, setting firm and impregnable boundaries to his energetic quests. He remembered long hours of being forced to "sit still" in a chair as punishment, and when he would challenge his parents' beliefs, the answer was usually, "That's just the way *we* think." The clear message was: "You should think that way too." Ron developed a fierce hatred for his stern and foreboding father, vowing to escape someday and outdo him. Which he did.

After leaving home, Ron did well in college and married an equally bright, energetic woman. He joined a marketing firm and experienced early success. About this time his father took ill with heart disease. Ron returned home to find this fearsome man weak and disabled, a shadow of the beast embedded in Ron's mind. They made some peace, but lacked the closeness Ron's brothers had with their father.

Ron's armor shattered. He began experiencing his successes with more caution, not trusting their staying power. Wracked with doubt, he became ineffective. He fought with his wife and she left abruptly, no longer recognizing the man she married. Ron sank into a bleak hopelessness, mastering his job, but never fulfilling the promise his early successes foretold.

In therapy, Ron focused on his father's failing health and the hatred he had always felt. Often, when he succeeded at work, he gleefully saw his father's disapproving face, only to put it aside in triumph. Soon, however, the strong, disapproving father was replaced by a frail and weakened man. Every victory seemed to damage the image more. Unconsciously, Ron was killing his father with each success. And the guilt was destroying him. He could avoid the guilt by avoiding success. His life floated in this compromise as he sought relief through treatment.

Ron's treatment was lengthy (two years) and incomplete (he could have benefited from a full analysis), but he was able to bring these images to the surface for open exploration. Through reality testing we disconnected Ron's successes from his father's illness, thus releasing the guilt that was sabotaging his career, and his life. At the time of termination (he was promoted out of state), Ron was relatively free of depression, dating actively, and able to be completely creative at work, though he had yet to fully make peace and friends with his father in the real world.

All men are neurotic to some degree. They struggle with the wish to win and fear the guilt that comes from winning. In the Vaillant study, the healthiest men in terms of coping skills had "out done" their parents in socio-economic status. They had channeled their drives, negotiated with their guilt, and won. Only a small percentage of men attain this without difficulty and most find varying ways to deal with guilt. The most common is to see the persecution or evil as emanating from "out there," rather than in their own heads. This form of "projecting evil" is common individually and in societies as a whole. Or, as Cormac McCarthy says in *The Crossing*:

"…As if the darkness had a soul itself that was the sun's assassin hurrying to the west as once men did believe, as they may believe again."

A good example of how machismo plays out in the real world versus our minds comes from the life of a world-renowned villain.

Carlos the Jackal: the most feared assassin of the twentieth century; the subject of movies, books, and folklore. He was brilliant, fearless, unstoppable. The ultimate killing machine.

"The Jackal" was taken into custody while under anesthesia for plastic surgery to remove his love handles. What? Life in hiding, you see, was not spent honing nerves of steel and lightning reflexes, but of indulgence in alcohol and gluttony. The undercover police video showed poor Carlos being mercilessly harassed by his girlfriend for "letting himself go," i.e., becoming a fat slob.

*The Day of the Jackal* was *our* creation of this hated and flawless killing machine. Carlos was a hired thug whose luck finally played out; a "supervillain" whose very human needs and frailties brought him in for justice. We created him for the same reason we created our superheroes—they are the embodiment of all good—while Gadhafi, Hussein, and Carlos are all bad. Ruthless, murderous, and incorrigible, *yes*; the embodiment of evil, *no*.

We identify with our heroes to elevate our own psyches from our flaws, and project our *own* ruthlessness and murderous wishes onto our villains. We can "fight" with our villains rather than with ourselves.

To see the Russians as the "source of evil in the world" (Reagan), is to create an enemy to be feared and fought rather than seeing *them* as being put together psychologically like *us*. Carlos the Jackal, the super assassin was (and is) a man disgustingly more similar to all men than we are comfortable in admitting. As Elisabeth Kubler Ross once said, "There's a little Hitler in all of us."

Of course, healthy, normal men wouldn't *consider* taking another's life (except if physically threatened or in war). Murder displays a lack of internal superego functioning and perhaps much deeper psychopathy. Still, Carlos is simply *not* a superman nor supervillain, nor is he terribly dissimilar from the rest of us.

## SOLUTIONS

Accepting primitive projections or outbursts without protest encourages their continuation. It also affects your own self-esteem. When the storm dies, approach your partner to discuss the *content* of his outburst, not the outburst itself. Be clear you will not accept being squelched down or abused, even though you are open to legitimate criticism. Be firm, but not threatening (a fine line), and be patient: most men aren't used to doing this. If you cannot achieve success, suggest a session with a neutral third party (a therapist!). Accept nothing less than being treated with respect and openness, being sure you reciprocate. Persistence remains your best tool.

- Help your man understand his own standards. These may be unconscious, but control most of his actions.
- Seek out a mate with compatible standards and values.
- Openly discuss guilt and spiritual issues. By discussing taboos, you open him up to himself *and* to you.
- Assess that guilt does not play too much or too little a role in his life.
- If having you triggers guilt, head for the door.

# CHECKLIST
# UNHEALTHY GUILT:

1). Does your man seem to self-sabotage? Not just now and then, but regularly?

2). Is he plagued by guilt—apologizing all the time?

3). When opportunity presents itself, does he pull away, explaining, "We already have enough"?

4). When confronted with inappropriate behavior does he respond with, "I'm just a bad person"? This may be a belief *and* an avoidance of responsibility

5). Does sex with you bring out conflicts of shame or guilt for his pleasure, which don't seem to be resolved?

6). Is he still a "child" in his father's presence, or act shy and inhibited around his mother?

7). Does he seem to deny guilt—openly testing rules and limits to show his lack of concern?

# CHECKLIST
# HEALTHY GUILT:

1). Does his income meet or exceed his father's? Our study of healthier men showed this to be almost universally true.

2). Do he and his father interact as adult friends, in a relatively equal relationship?

3). Do he and his mother experience open and mutually enjoyable pleasure in each other's company?

4). Is his spiritual life based on loving acceptance and openness rather than rigid rules and punishment?

5). Does he experience sex with you with joy and passion, without conflicts?

6). When treated unfairly does he confront the person openly?

7). Does he pursue his dreams? A man must be content with his guilt to be free to see the horizon.

## QUESTIONS AND ANSWERS

1). Question: My husband is very successful and a real up-and-comer. However, his father developed cancer, and is dying. Now, my husband hangs around the house, morose and not talking. What can I do?

Answer: Encourage him to talk about his father and begin grieving his loss. He must arrive at the conclusion that it's "not his fault" on his own, but an open ear allows him to verbalize feelings. Insist on his return to work. Suggest couple's or individual therapy if he resists.

2). Question: My husband blames everyone else that he's not being promoted quickly enough, when I *know* it's because he won't play company politics. Now, I'm even afraid he might *lose* his job. How can I get through to him?

Answer: Be tactful but direct about your observations, careful *not* to come across as another attacker. Offer a friendly voice, but don't buy into his strategy of blame. And don't argue it's the other's fault when it's not.

3). Question: When I try and discuss hurt feelings with my boyfriend, he turns it all around—denying, accusing, then focusing on his own feelings. How can I get him to deal with *me* and *my* needs?

Answer: In a non-threatening or accusing way, redirect him back to *your* concerns. Let him know you are very interested in his problems, but insist on your own time first. Never accept a denial or accusation you feel isn't true, but offer your observations in a kind, helpful way.

4). Question: My man has a tendency to act like a jerk and shows *no* remorse. What gives?

Answer: In adolescence through young adulthood, the standard is revoked to allow gratification of the sexual and aggressive drives ("all is fair in love and war"), often allowing a man *with* standards to become promiscuous. Society's lessening of rigidity also promotes these behaviors. A healthy man, when committed, will experience guilt and not "like" himself when he transgresses these barriers. Accept nothing less.

5). Question: My boyfriend transgresses in little ways: lying to his boss, stealing small things from work, covering up little errors. Is this indicative of a deeper problem, or is it just little white lies? Should I be concerned?

Answer: Small transgressions that form a definite pattern *do* mean something. He may not be willing to face up to it until it causes pain in the real world. This may be a sign of a deeper problem; time will tell.

6). Question: My husband is thirty-five and still terrified of his father. Though he denies it, he never crosses the man. It makes me crazy as sometimes this really interferes in *our* life. Am I being selfish?

Answer: Your husband is classically neurotic, still conflicted with the original object. He needs to break away both physically and psychologically to enjoy life (and for you to enjoy yours). It is not selfish to want more from a marriage than this.

7). Question: We are in our late twenties, happily married, with a two-year-old daughter. My husband is loving and devoted, but several times a week has long phone conversations with his mother, just for "chit-chat." Isn't this one of those Oedipal things? Should I be jealous?

Answer: His enjoyment in talking with his mother is likely, in fact, "pre-genital," and what he seeks is nurturing. Few adult men openly lust for their mothers. Your response should be based on whether he favors her over you as the central point. The best "chit-chat" should always be yours. Proceed with caution however, as mothers and daughters-in-law are natural enemies and unnecessary conflict should be avoided. *If* conflict ensures, make sure he chooses you.

8). Question: My ex-husband allows our six-year-old daughter to sleep in the same bed with him on the weekends. Our divorce was bitter and I don't want to cause a fight unless I have to , but isn't this unhealthy?

Answer: Unless your ex-husband is a pedophile, the "horrible" scenario can be avoided. It may be calming for each of them, and have little impact on him, but your daughter is likely over-stimulated. Approach him about the impact on her. Good boundaries help bring closure to the Oedipal Phase in the best way possible, even in divorced or blended families.

9). Question: I was sexually abused as a child and have to be approached gently to enjoy sex. My husband occasionally has been too hasty, causing me to feel panicked. *Now* he is reluctant to approach me. How can I help him?

Answer: Your husband likely cares for you deeply enough to feel guilt when his sex drive causes you pain. Approach him gingerly, but invitingly, making sure he understands your sensitivities. Couple's work would be helpful.

10). Question: My husband was raised in a fundamentalist home. Recently we've suffered severe economic setbacks. He has reacted by *increasing* our tithe! When I ask, he quotes scripture. What might this mean?

Answer: It sounds as though your husband suffers from a harsh, primitive superego with exaggerated guilt that was enhanced by his upbringing. He is likely "tithing" to avoid further perceived setbacks. Approach this gently, if at all, as my experience has been that it's difficult to argue with someone's belief system once it is well entrenched.

*Chapter Four*

# The Fourth Key:
# The Need for Other Men

*"Our stories are intertwined in the DNA*
*of our friendship."*
—Sam Keene, *Fire in the Belly.*

## THE MYTH OF MALE BONDING

Men have a pronounced need to be with other men. Women tend to respond to this statement in two ways:
1). That it's stating the obvious, as women's need to be with women is both conscious and unconflicted. Or, 2). They question the very existence of this need in men, based on their man's behavior, as male friendships play out quite differently from their female counterparts.

This need in men is, unfortunately, largely unconscious and variably conflicted, depending upon the man.

But the importance of male friendships cannot be overestimated. Men who have them live fuller, richer lives. They also live longer and healthier, according to the Vaillant study. Outcome data on hospitalized adolescents revealed that the single best predictor of a good outcome five years after discharge was relationship with peers. This overrode all other factors, including relationships with doctors, nurses, or family.

In Richard Ford's *The Sportswriter*, we witness the painful, empty angst of the middle-aged male. Women are plentiful, but elusive as Frank Bascombe can attest. He can't maintain a relationship with any of the available women. He strains to connect with men, but friendships are shallow or threatening and he winds up alone and confused, in the end relating to no one. His intelligence and ability to articulate cannot bridge the gap as he describes in exasperation, "Words, my oldest friend and ally, fail me," just prior to receiving a relationship-ending left hook from his girlfriend.

A man must reach peace with himself before friendships and romance can be enjoyed at their deepest level. However, as with many of man's other needs, the expression of this often takes complicated forms.

The intensity of male bonding occurs during the latency period—between the resolution of the Oedipus and adolescence. "Latency" is a relative term, and anyone who has contact with six-to- twelve-year-olds will challenge this as a quiet time. It is *relative* only in that the oedipal resolution brings a temporary lull into the deeper psychosexual development, which is then kicked back into high gear with adolescence. During latency, boys attach and learn how to relate to other boys.

In the almost archetypal coming-of-age movie, *Stand By Me* (based upon the Stephen King short story), four latency-age boys have journeyed out on a quest. Sitting around the campfire, "…we talked into the night, the kind of talk that seemed important until you discovered girls." It is the presence of girls and ultimately competition that breaks male bonding, though it never really goes away.

Of course, other activities occur during latency, such as increasing physical development and intellectual powers. In fact, an estimated seventy percent of retained facts in adult life were learned in latency! (Who was the first President of the United States? What is the capitol of South Dakota?) This shows what men's minds *can* do when not thinking about sex.

For boys, the main issues of this time center around developing friendships, rules, and social order. Girls have "cooties" and are avoided if at all possible (and vice-versa). Once, however, a girl can show she *too* is in latency (tomboy), she can be accepted. A "kissy" girl is not invited back to the club.

The remnants of these attitudes remain in adult life as well. Hunting camps or sports bars change drastically when a woman arrives. Harmony is disrupted and companions become competitors. In these places women are still treated as sex objects (i.e., foldouts or pinups), or as completely nonexistent. The satirist Joe Bob Briggs, commenting on the demise of the male gym as opposed to the new spas said, "Gyms do not have a picture of Victoria Principal in her leotards by the door. Gyms have a picture of Floyd Patterson, training for the Liston fight. It's usually hanging over the cigarette machine."

The reason for this expulsion of women is simple: to distance the possibility of a real woman presenting a threat. Most boys clubs during latency have as rule one: NO GIRLS.

The most severe example of "girl phobia" occurs within military units or in olden times with ships at sea. These represent the last hallows of latency clubs in adult life, and are poor substitutes for the mature hunter-gatherer bands of our ancestors. Considered bad luck to sailors where decreased morale and loss of teamwork could spell death, women were often declared witches and thrown overboard. So when your man is playing cards or watching the game with his buddies, enter the room carefully!

Do you think this doesn't happen today? In July of 1994, a Federal District judge ruled that Shannon Faulkner could, indeed, attend The Citadel (South Carolina's all-male military school) as a full-fledged cadet.

Retired Lieut. Col. T. Nugent Courvoisie, seventy-seven (who was immortalized as The Citadel's harsh taskmaster, The Bear, in Pat Conroy's best seller, *The Lord's of Discipline*), said in response to the ruling:

"That girl says she wants to come in and be one of the boys. But the minute she comes in, the atmosphere changes. She ruins the whole concept of getting everyone together and working on the same team."

Although the statement is quite politically incorrect, there is on a very primal level some truth to it for men who make male bonding their primary attachments.

Male bonding in fact *protects* men from the conflicts stimulated when women are present. A latency-age boy has renounced his mother as a love object and identified with old Dad, now no longer a blood rival, but a mentor (hopefully). Attachment is met through men, castration is not an active issue as sex is taboo, and guilt is avoided by following internal and societal standards. And whether this bonding occurs between friends or brothers, the effects remain and filter through a man's entire life.

*Jamaica, long ago;*

*We arise each morning before dawn to swim out to the reef. My brothers and I know the fish are sluggish now—our best chance to spear lunch. Dad often accompanies us, and sometimes Johnny, the huge Jamaican who lifeguards up the beach.*

*Yesterday I took my turn with the spear and mistakenly shot a puffer fish. Within seconds, it blew up as big as a beach ball on the end of my spear. We ate ham sandwiches for lunch.*

*Today dawns calm and cloudless as the morning sun plays on the waves and spray and brightly colored fish. Don points to a slow-moving yellowtailed snapper. Mike spears him cleanly—fish for lunch. The rising sun warms our backs as we swim to shore.*

*Four months later, Mike was dead and I was never to know his physical presence again. But he lives with me through my memories, which will only die when I do. And sometimes, late at night when it's very quiet, we swim out to the reef.*

Latency is truly the eye of the storm, preparing for the turmoil of adolescence. While in it, boys' friendships flourish in an unconflicted manner. But, as the narrator says at the end of *Stand By Me*: "I never had any friends later on like the ones I had when I was twelve. Jesus, does anybody?"

While women cannot usually relate to this statement, men understand it quite well.

A male, no longer identifying with his mother (the female), also distances himself from feminine traits such as intimacy and vulnerability, which threaten his masculinity. Add to that the links (both conscious and unconscious) between weakness, intimacy, vulnerability, fear, and sexual insecurities to male homosexuality, and the stage is set for men to maintain distance in their same-sex friendships.

In adult life, healthy men attach to a woman and their own families. They maintain bonding connections with other men through work, sports (either participatory or as a spectator), hunting, partying, or even military connections (army buddies or reserves). These activities are healthy and, for most men, necessary. For some, they are the primary bonds—in 1975, Larry Fine and Moe Howard of *The Three Stooges* died within six months of each other.

In truth, male bonding still exists, and remains vitally important to men. The form it takes from here on out, however, becomes obtuse.

In Texas, the cowboy mystique endures. Tall in the saddle, violently independent and self-sufficient, a man could survive on his wits and skills in a foreboding country. Of course, he spent virtually all of his time with other cowboys, causing the speculation that he was a repressed homosexual.

Larry McMurtry points out in *In a Narrow Grave: Essays on Texas*, that this man is in fact a repressed *heterosexual*; skilled, patient, and determined with his horse, but terrified around women. In a developmental sense, he is frozen at the stage of pre-adolescent bonding, where skills are honed, friendships most intense, and women scarce. Counter-phobic behavior becomes a lifestyle and fears of incompetence with women and guilt are avoided.

The lure is strong, however, as few men (including me!) would turn down the offer to join Gus, Call, and the boys in driving the herd to Montana in *Lonesome Dove*.

Or, as described in contemporary terms by Thor Heyerdahl (preparing the *Kon Tiki* voyage) in a oneword cable to his companions: "Come." The reply: "Coming."

The "myth" part of male bonding then, needs to be understood not in terms of fiction, but rather, in its true meaning. A myth is the collective dream of a culture that helps explain the life passages of men; it is, as many have said, the story of the wisdom of life.

And those men who can overcome their other fears and bond in a meaningful way often provide sustenance for relationships that last a lifetime.

"There's a bright golden haze on the meadow," the aging composer said, wiping a tear from his eye. "These were the most beautiful words I had ever seen and I knew my collaboration with Oscar would be successful." —Richard Rogers on his first coauthorship with Oscar Hammerstein in *Oklahoma!*

## THE TRIBAL MALE

*"...The Australopithecine troop wakes as the sun rises, individuals in their sleeping places in trees or along cliff-like perches, relatively safe from nighttime predators. Slowly they clamber to the ground to the accompaniment of scattered vocalizations and*

*occasional skirmishes, the unfinished business of the previous day's social interactions...*

*"Several neighboring Australopithecine troops had been spotted during the day, provoking alarm calls between them."*
—Richard Leakey, *Origins Revisited.*

*"...Sounds like training camp for the Oakland Raiders!"*
—Dinner companion, under his breath at the Dallas Gala honoring Dr Leakey.

Since hunter-gatherer tribes first formed, banding together with shared responsibilities and spoils, men have needed to function as a unit. Hunting, making war, and choosing mates all required a hierarchy of relationship that allowed each man to develop his own skills, and his need to dominate as well as articulate within the whole.

We are genetically identical to these men and our psyches are constructed in the same way.

Nearness to men allows an attachment that gratifies the pre-genital (maternal) need to be close to another person. It also gives a healthy outlet to the normal homosexual feelings present in all men. The hierarchy or pecking order ensures minimal overt conflict or violence, and can actually help protect from castration fears if your tribe can avoid domination by another one.

Wars between tribes once served a very useful purpose. They established hunting and at times, breeding territories while *rarely* exposing anyone to real dangers of injury or death. American Indians counted coup to score a battle—who symbolically humiliated whom. Not until modern weaponry provided man a means of mass killing did war take on the grisly proportions it has today.

Historians now point to the American Civil War as the last remnants of "noble" war, where men fought *mano-y-mano* for honor and grace. Throughout the ranks of enlisted men up to its generals, the male need to dominate, as well as an undying loyalty to other men, surfaced. The evidence of this remained until the very last days of the war.

The Southern soldiers themselves would not concede defeat. "The few men who still carried muskets were a ragtaggled bunch ...yet still, they were waiting for General Lee to tell them where to turn and fight." —from Ken Burns' *The Civil War.*

Were these men merely fighting for the honor of the South? Or did an intense loyalty to the father figure of Robert E. Lee play a part? Or perhaps was it simply their love for each other?

As finally the surrender became inevitable, Lee said, "There is nothing for me to do but go and see General Grant. And I would rather die a thousand deaths."

Almost one hundred years later, the twentieth-century warrior General George S. Patton summed up this sentiment more succinctly, if less poetically: "No bastard ever won a war by dying for his country. He won it by making the other poor, dumb bastard die for his country."

War strikes a piercing chord in the hearts of men—it is male bonding at its most intense, where the price for mistakes is death. Someone with whom you have shared a foxhole remains a blood brother for life.

*Washington D.C., a clear, autumn day:*

*I walk down Pennsylvania Avenue, feeling uneasy while passing the war veterans working as vendors who implore me to remember them, and those who didn't return. Their souls, which speak from their eyes, appear wounded, betrayed.*

*I come to The Wall, and all of the names. It builds slowly at first then towers over my head; a crushing wave of young men now dead, lost forever save in memory.*

*I feel the tug all men of my generation so painfully feel. My tribe had gone to battle and I did not go; would not have gone. Drawing a high number saved me the choice, but in my heart, I knew nothing was at stake in Southeast Asia worth my dying for.*

*Did I betray them, this mountain of dead young men, never to see as I do the gleam in their children's eyes on a Christmas day, or watch a spaniel freeze to point on a bright winter's afternoon? Or did they*

*betray me, dying in what now seems a pointless cause,*
*their lives never again part of my generation of men?*

I lost an uncle I never knew at D-Day, and would
have bravely joined him given the chance. But we
were denied that clear kind of conflict. Of course, the
feminists now say it is this pull in young men that
creates the atmosphere which produces war in the first
place. This cannot be argued. But right or wrong,
moral or not, this conflict created a wound for men of
my time that does not heal.

War heroes strike a chord in all men as well. We
remember the brave and the martyrs, but a hero
represents the struggle within all men. "Cowards die
many times before their deaths; the valiant never taste
of death but once," Shakespeare told us from the
sixteenth century. Or, as William Wallace said in
*Braveheart*, "All men die, but not all men truly live."

I have never met a truly "valiant" man as *all* men
die through their own fears many thousands of times.
Valiance represents sublimation of the drive in order
to gain control in the real world. It is also a counter-
phobic defense to undo castration fears.

Chuck Yeager gave a vivid description of what it's
like in actual combat for fighter pilots, the forbearers
of the *Right Stuff* and the ego ideal of his day. He told
of men freezing-up in combat, unable to respond.
Some defecated in their flight suits. In one kill, a
German officer bailed out upon seeing Yeager, the
plane effectively downed with no shots fired. This is

the norm—a human reaction to the reality of death. Valiance is a rare commodity, and must be balanced with judgment to serve a man's best interest.

War causes men to bond for survival. And men's ancient need to depend upon one another in times of crisis infiltrates present-day life. A man's experiences of the world and its dangers are very real. Although these dangers are expressed differently now from in more primitive times, the essence has not changed.

*Ioni Creek, The Brazos River:*

*We drift slowly past the confluence of the Ioni Creek where it blends into the Brazos. On the ledge, under the big live oak, John Graves shot and ate game, inspiring boys such as us to float and explore.*

*Long ago, two close friends were attacked by Comanches here, and separated from one another. One died and the other lived. The survivor carried with him a haunting plea. Did his friend yell, "Run for it," or, "Fight for it."?*

*My friend Danny and I camp there in a blinding rainstorm. We cook outside with cedar as fuel; wet but nourished.*

*Many, many years later:*

*I wait at the gravesite until everyone leaves. The gravediggers begin their work of lowering Danny into the ground to cover him with dirt. I drop my rose on the casket and wait until the workers engage their task. They shoot me curious looks.*

*You see, through our many discussions of life and death, I know Danny would want me to make sure some gravedigger didn't drop him on his head. It was our bond. A bond forged over so many years of nights on the Brazos River, sharing our hearts while counting falling stars. I leave his memory there, along with those two other, true friends who parted long ago; separate yet eternally bound; forever a part of my mind, a part of me.*

Most men ask to be buried next to their wives or mothers. But for some, the greatest attachment is to those beside whom they fought. Many men ask to be buried in military cemeteries. On his deathbed, Robert E. Lee returned to his men. His last words: "Strike the tent."

Still, you say, my man has no tribe and isn't at war for hunting or breeding rights. Though this may certainly appear so, the need still flourishes, and so, too, does its expression.

Every culture nurtures the myth of the warrior. The greatest honor that can be bestowed on a young man is to die in battle for his tribe or country. A walk through the Arlington National Cemetery attests to this fact. It is ancient, and goes to the very core of our beings.

A Viking who dies with sword in hand went straight to Valhalla. In Islam, a soldier killed in a

*Jihad* automatically enters paradise (a difficult task otherwise). Even in the future, we see Klingons attribute the only honorable death as one in battle. Why is this myth so powerful?

A man who dies in battle is killed at the peak of his manhood—*at his best*. With muscles taut he charges, fearless, next to his brethren in his finest hour, his fullest measure as a man. If he is victorious, this memory remains fixed. If he dies, it is "being all that he can be," and ends in glory.

In Michner's *Centennial*, the aging chief, Lame Beaver, faces an imminent battle with a neighboring tribe. He stakes his foot to a tethered pole so that his fear will not betray him and he will have an honorable death.

The warrior experiences the full force of his aggressive drive without conflict or social condemnation. He bonds with his peers. The pull is very powerful and is often sublimated into team sports or other group efforts. It remains at the heart of all mass conflicts, and can be used either powerfully or corruptly.

"It is a good day to fight, a good day to die. Brave hearts to the front. Weak hearts and cowards to the rear. Mount your ponies!" — Chief Crazy Horse, to his Lakota Sioux and Cheyenne warriors, upon learning of the presence of a column of blue coats approaching his camp on the Little Big Horn River, June 25, 1876. (As reported by Black Elk in the 1920s.) Within two hours, General George Armstrong

Custer and all the soldiers accompanying him from the 7th Cavalry were killed and their bodies dismembered so they could not enter the next world as whole men.

So what is the modern expression of this phenomenon? A man's firm or company may take on this role. Or, more likely, his "team."

I have become involuntarily attached to several teams as my own extended tribe, as have most men. The Cowboys of Dallas symbolically "count coup" with the Eagles of Philadelphia or the Giants of New York every blessed Sunday in the fall. I relish the victories and feel the wounds of each defeat. Of course, I have no *real* connection with the Dallas Cowboys—it's only in my head. But through the miracle of modern electronics, I can join my adoptive clan at will. And never lose one drop of blood!

I can argue for hours about the advantages of the slash-and-pursue defense as opposed to the old flex. When Roger Staubach was inducted into the Hall of Fame, I felt the pride of lifetime accomplishment. Of course, Mr Staubach wouldn't know me from Adam, but I was *there* for eleven years of Sundays, as Captain Comeback waged his wars and drew victory from the jaws of defeat. Through the Cowboys' woes of the late '80s (and now again in the late '90s), I grew befuddled when distant friends asked of the "Boys" ills.

Although I quit playing football in the ninth grade, and the only role I could possibly have, Team Psychiatrist, is already taken, I can use my team as an adoptive tribe to bolster my ego, as well as feel attached to a greater clan. And as *you* know, I am not alone.

Watching sports from all angles, in slow motion and with instant replay, is how many men join a tribe or clan. This can be relatively harmless (I don't watch if I have something better to do) or can, as with anything else in a man's mind, take on exaggerated importance.

Some men watch three games in a row every Saturday and Sunday, or spend all of the family's disposable income on tickets, regardless of the cost to others. I have patients who become profoundly depressed when their team loses (vicarious "wounds" should heal in approximately the length of a commercial) and obsess and ruminate for hours about contests into which they have no input. What's happening here?

To understand, we must leave the discussion of tribes and delve into the psychology of the hero. In each of us, an idealized object plays a specific and much-needed role in early life. The awareness that we are small and weak is terrifying. But we are attached to someone stronger and larger—godlike. This person physically protects us but also, his psychic image in our minds gives comfort. Depending upon life experiences and each person's individual capacity to fuse objects, some remnant of this phenomenon remains.

I cannot run the ball like O.J. Simpson, but I can *identify* with him when he does. He is endowed with that godlike aura, originally found in my mind at an early age. Of course, when O.J. then looks *very* human during his ordeal, my psyche is perplexed.

That *can't* be The Juice sitting there looking frightened and dazed, accused of murder and more. I've winced through the low-ball comedies as O.J. mumbled inane lines, and tolerated the rent-a-car commercials. But the *real* O.J. (the one preserved in my mind): It's third and long on a snowy Buffalo day with the game in the balance. The Juice explodes off left tackle, through the line, evading linebackers and safeties and surging into the endzone. Of course, I preserve the image for what it gives to *me*, not as a realistic assessment of the man. I reality-test, reminding myself that he is, after all, just a man, a man from a damaged past and chaotic present. He's not what *I* needed him to be.

In treating professional athletes, the first thing I've noticed is how different they are from what people expect. By and large, these are usually highly paid man-children, whose position in life fosters a belief that the rules for others don't apply to them. Disaster befalls anyone who carries this belief into real life. O.J. Simpson played football well; the rest was my (our) creation.And how the mighty do fall. All around.

"When I hit a guy, I want his head to come off—I want to see heads roll." —Dick Butkus, 1960s middle-linebacker, Chicago Bears. Most-feared player (or human being) of his era.

"Tastes Great!" (or is it, "Less Filling"?) —Dick Butkus, beer salesman, wearing a shit-eating grin, 1980s. We tolerate these transgressions because we "knew him when." He still keeps our respect, though feared no more.

Idealization does have useful value. The idealized person is usually *better* at something (or many things) than I am. He is not only stronger, but nicer, or more normal, less selfish. It helps me to strive for these things. Of course, in real life there are no heroes, only illusions we created. This reality-testing is powerful for men, and opens the opportunity to "be your own hero"—one of the final steps in autonomy.

As Joseph Campbell said, "The hero is the one who comes to *participate* in life courageously and decently..." (Italics mine.)

A man who is unable to reality-test, or spends too much of his time in front of the tube is attempting to compensate for real or imagined dangers by futile means. He is participating in vicarious or surrogate achievement, which is not at all the same thing.

Not that active participation is always the best choice. Following the Leon Spinks/Muhammed Ali fight, where Spinks won a surprise upset, a commemorative video of the fight was made available for seventy-five dollars. Fight fans could relive this classic battle between these larger-than-life beings in the comfort of their own living rooms. Upon hearing of this offering, Mr Spinks' agent remarked, "Hell, for seventy-five dollars, Leon will come out to your home!" On second thought, I'll just watch the video.

Participatory sports, however, are psychologically and physically *much* healthier than electronic sports viewing. With diminishing skills, many men stop playing shortly after college. A man who is active must overcome the narcissistic result and perceived castration of "poor performance." Humor, as always, helps, as a forty-and-over participant in the Dallas Hoop-It-Up said, "Basketball at this age is kinda like sex—you don't have to be good at it to have fun."
To be active a man must also seek out like-minded men (or women!) and put in the extra effort needed to function physically (as required by age).     Men who do this live longer, are emotionally healthier, and make better mates.

As the track athlete on a relay team in a (healthier) beer commercial says, "We always run faster together."

Sports in our culture also provide a good forum for Father/Son relationships. Like the soldiers looking to General Lee for orders, boys (and men) look to coaches for orders. In all of life, boys need grown men to help them become men themselves.

Robert Bly's thesis in *Iron John* is that without fathers or substitutes as mentors, boys grow up without role models and have "empty space" inside that eventually gets filled with "evil." The connection with Iron John is that boys need proper mentors to become men and *safely* be in touch with their "wild men," i.e., to handle the power.

Boys *do* need men around in order to become men themselves. Bly's point that in modern society, even intact families lack male leadership (6 p.m.: "I'm tired from work") is extremely accurate. As we discussed in Chapter Three, the boy needs a strong father to "bounce off of" in order to have adequate superego functioning (*guilt* modulation). A son also loves his father and wishes for his approval (ego ideal), and feels shame if he does not live up to "the" standard. After the Oedipal Phase, a boy *identifies* psychologically with his father (if you can't beat 'em, join 'em), emulating his style and behavior. You need a father (or stand in) present to accomplish these tasks.

I've seen "healthy" fatherless children search for a father. That person can be Marshall Dillon or a distant relative. In other cultures, the extended family may serve as the ego ideal.

The "wild man" inside of us, "covered in water" (the unconscious) is also a theme in Hesse's writings (*Steppenwolf*: cultured man cannot handle inner urges and becomes "wolf" at night), as well as in *The Lord of the Rings* (wear the ring of power too long and be corrupted). The point being your *Id* is too powerful to touch, but must be accessed to be truly alive. Freud describes the relationship of the ego to the id as a rider on a runaway horse, struggling to stay aboard and gain control. Do not look directly into the sun, or like Icarus, fly too close, or catastrophe will ensue.

A father, father figure, or tribe all help a man to reality-test, and find his place in the grand scheme of things. Father and son relationships take many forms, and aid the boy or man in death as well as life.

*Fort Worth, Texas:*
*The ambulance flies into the night. My oldest brother lies on the stretcher in the back, burned beyond recognition. I sit, frightened and confused, in the front seat with my other brother, Don.*

*"How bad am I hurt?" Mike asks our father.*

*"Pretty bad, son," Dad answers, calm and direct—no time to pull punches.*

*"I'll try my best to stay alive."*

*These are the last words I knew my brother to say.*

Through friendships, tribal connections, war, and sports, men bond with men. There is another important way in which men bond, both with actual men, and with the metaphor of all mankind. It is through an activity that disgusts and abhors most women. But as Joseph Campbell put it so well:

"Neither in body nor in mind do we inhabit the world of those hunting races of the Paleolithic millennia, to whose lives and life ways we nevertheless owe the very forms of our bodies and structures of our minds. Memories of their animal envoys still sleep, somehow, within us; for they wake a little and stir when we venture into wilderness."

## HUNTING

During hunting season, my wife and daughters used to say in unison, "That's barbaric. You're going out to slaughter small animals and eat them!"

I was defenseless. Because of course, it was true.

No longer needed to attain food, hunting is now considered "sport." But regardless of your protests and very logical arguments, the urge to hunt remains. A recent *USA Today* report stated that sixty million Americans hunt or fish.

Hunting is an activity women seem to have the greatest difficulty in understanding. In fact, men who do not grow up in hunting cultures have problems adapting to it in adult life, simply because it is a brutal activity, with large amounts of blood. But rest assured, in places where hunting isn't available, other activities (i.e., ice hockey in the northeast) substitute. Why would a sophisticated, cultured, educated, sensitive man engage in such primitive activity?

The taking of an animal in the field is a savage, gory act. It is also, next to sexual fulfillment, probably the most gratifying activity in a man's life. How could this be? The answer is both complicated and simple.

Human beings evolved to hunt. The aggressive instinct lies in every living person, and, even if sublimated, remains evident in all thoughts, feelings, and activities. It exists to ensure the survival of the species, to attain food, assert dominance for breeding, and establish home territory. Distasteful though it may be, there lives a beast within us all.

The hunter/gatherer tribes of many thousand years ago were genetically identical to us now. In the social order of these tribes, men hunted in bands while women remained behind caring for the young and gathering food. This system worked until the advent of modern agriculture and the domestication of animals.

In modern hunter/gatherer tribes (such as the !Kung San people of southern Africa), a curious breakdown emerges when behaviors are analyzed. In spite of all the sound and fury, only about forty percent of the tribe's nutritional needs get met by the male hunters. Female gatherers provide the majority of the food, basically collected in their spare time. Another need seems to be at work here.

Hunting is an intensely social activity for men. Some hunting (deer, large game) usually requires the actual shooting to be done alone, but there is always a camp or at least men back home with whom to share the kill (thus the trophy mount on the wall). This is, of course, penis measuring in pure form as men compare weapons, kills, and potency while bonding with fellow men in a nebulous, unconflicted way. As we talked about rules in Chapter Three, Guilt, woe be to him who wins but breaks the rules. In the same manner, the unsporting kill is despised.

*"Never trust a man until you've seen him shoot at something dangerous or that he wants really badly at fifty yards or under."*
—Ernest Hemingway, *True at First Light*

William Faulkner spoke of hunting in *The Bear* as a rite of passage *necessary* for young men. He claimed it taught patience and humility, and lamented the loss of the wilderness as a testing ground for youth.

It is worthy to note that after Faulkner's hero participated in the kill of the book's namesake, the next chapter finds him anxiously "under the covers" with a woman. One preceded the other. This story also dealt with the rules of honor in hunting, as a successful hunt meant you hunted well, not necessarily productively. In the end, all is reduced to its most primitive elements as Boone—the man who sleeps with dogs—is the only one capable of killing the bear, and does so with raw spiritual energy and his bare hands.

Man evolved through this history. I have felt the calmest and most at one with my environment during times I have been hunting with other men. It is a primal activity, and one in which the connection to our ancient ancestors wells up within us. As Robert Bly described this activity in *Iron John*, "...a boy is mythologically living through the past history of man, which includes century after century of joyful hunting."

This activity connects man to all of mankind, while assuaging other fears as well. Hunting undoes castration anxiety. A man's "gun" is potent and competent. He communes with other men, bonding in a relatively unconflicted way. By following the rules, the aggressive instinct is satisfied while avoiding guilt. And he finds spiritual oneness with "mother earth" by fulfilling his role in the food chain. Barbaric, yes, but deeply gratifying.

As Sam Keene said in *Fire in the Belly*:

"From the study of the few hunting and gathering societies that have survived into modern times, we know that when men live by hunting a three-way mystical bond grows up between them and the animals upon which they depend. First, the hunter identifies with the animal—the bear, the bison, the eland— that he must kill. The Bushmen, for instance, believe that they were previously springbok, and that their spirit continues to live in the spirit world with the eternal springbok. Many hunters take animal names. Second, the hunter must communicate with the mind of the animal both to understand its way so he can stalk it successfully and to receive permission to 'sacrifice' it. Third, the hunter identifies his manhood both with his totem animal and with the instrument of his craft....

His penis partakes of the power of the spear, the arrow, the gun with which he kills and provides food to the tribe."

Yes, women find hunting disgusting. I have met a few women who enjoy hunting, many who tolerate it, but most wish their men would not behave this way. Be aware, however, that unless your man plays power forward for the Knicks, there are few better ways of channeling aggressions. Besides, other women don't venture into the hunting camp—a fairly harmless activity. Eat the meat with gusto— that is how it was taken.

*Late Fall, Cloudcroft, New Mexico:*
*We have ridden hard since before dawn and are returning to the ranch house, exhausted and empty handed. My dad and I are joined by my mother as we collapse behind the barn to watch the fading New Mexico sunset.*

*Suddenly, the largest animal I have ever seen in the wild appears. A mule deer, as big as a small pony, comes at a swift trot fully one quarter of a mile away. My heart pounds as Dad and I empty our guns; an improbable shot at best. The deer goes down.*

*We run to him. One bullet went clean through the heart—the shooter unknowable. Stunned by the sheer size of the beast, we stare in the sepia light for a long moment. Then my father says, unblinkingly, "Good shot, son."*

A brutal and barbaric show of unnecessary death in a land of mass-produced plenty? Undoubtedly. But a rite of passage nonetheless, and a moment in time I carry with me each day. The real question is, where do young men have this type of crystallizing experience in the wild today? Perhaps Faulkner was right.

*Iredell, TX. Bosque County:*
*"Uncle Gawee—look!" My nephew, Mitch, can barely contain himself as a lone dove flies close to our "stand" under a huge oak tree. Mitch plugs his ears as I shoot and the bird crumples.*

*Mitch, Nicholas, and Jill squeal with glee, racing madly to where the dove has fallen, all wildly overrunning our deceased prey in their exuberance. This is, however, some minor redemption for me as I missed the last two birds to questions of, "Are you losing your touch, Uncle Gawee?"*

*The Texas sun sets magnificently behind the two-hundred-year-old live oaks as the September heat relents to the cool of early evening. Granny will have dinner waiting back at the cabin. The bonding of clans, through hunting rituals as old as human existence, links us to our genetic and spiritual forbearers. As I walk in the greyness of dusk and see the glow of the cabin lights, I am at one with my clan, my primitive ancestors, and myself.*

So indeed, men need other men, both literally and metaphorically. Our stories are most certainly intertwined in the DNA of our friendships, as Sam Keene so eloquently said. And these stories stay with us to the end of our days.

They help us to understand ourselves, to feel connected, to "be at one."

Norman Maclean wrote of the bonds between father and son and brother to brother in his beautiful, quiet story, *A River Runs Through It*. Ostensibly a novella about fly fishing, this activity becomes the backdrop to a rhapsody of the bonds between men to one another, and to nature. As Maclean concluded:

"Of course, now I am too old to be much of a fisherman, and now of course I usually fish the big waters alone, although some friends think I shouldn't... In the Arctic halflight of the canyon, all existence fades to a being with my soul and memories and the sounds of the Big Blackfoot River and a four-count rhythm and the hope that a fish will rise.

"Eventually, all things merge into one, and a river runs through it...."

# CASE STUDY

*"They say you are not you except in terms of other people ...because what you do, which is what you are, only has meaning in relation to other people."*
—Robert Penn Warren, *All the King's Men.*

### Rodney

Rodney came into treatment after a poor review at work. As a forty-five-year-old businessman, he had been extremely successful in public relations and sales, and found himself in the unusual role of facing a bad review with career-altering implications. No one questioned his skills, effort, or dedication: he simply didn't fit in with senior management, his next step up.

After the initial assessment, Rodney divulged that he was, in fact, very depressed. It had subtly haunted him for years, but he always managed to brush it aside, filling the emptiness he felt with work and family. He had a dedicated if superficial marriage, and two daughters with whom he spent time but didn't deeply connect. He had no true male friends. Rodney was lonely.

The only child of a successful business couple, Rodney's family had moved a great deal. His dad was distant and preoccupied, rarely having time for him. His mother was also either absent or depressed, and often Rodney would negotiate with repairmen or domestic help as they came to the house. These skills blossomed in his adult life. He could negotiate deals with relative strangers swiftly and deftly. His frequent moves left few close friends. He could recall none by name in our interviews.

As we went, I learned more of his problems at work. "Senior Management" consisted of "good ol' boys": golfing and partying together as well as family outings. Rodney could connect with a stranger in record time, but was uncomfortable and out of place in an afternoon golf foursome. His discomfort showed and his boss would have none of it.

Rodney decided to consult his father about his dilemma, something he'd never before attempted. His father was, by all accounts, a good businessman. But here we learn something important about Rodney's development: his father felt uncomfortable in trying to establish camaraderie with his adult child. Eventually, however, the two strangers broke down barriers, talking openly of their business frustrations and reminiscing (for the first time) about their life together. Rodney's conflict in closeness with his father paralleled his ability to break down his defensiveness with me, trusting a man with his vulnerabilities for the first time.

He began talking more with his neighbor, even inviting him to play golf. Within a few months, his loneliness seemed less personal as simple openness with other men filled an old empty place in his life.

He began to talk of his anger at his parents for not putting *his* needs high on their priority list, something he hoped not to repeat with his own children. His marriage became closer.

Unfortunately for Rodney, the changes were too late for his firm, and he was passed over for a career-making promotion. He was, however, able to make a move to a smaller, but potentially more-profitable company with much greater career-advancement opportunities. The move threatened his vow to his children, but he made certain to attend to their needs in the transition. He accepted a referral for continued treatment in his new home town.

Rodney's situation demonstrates how a man's need for male friendships can impact his life, and how the lack of them do as well. As he learned to relate to other men, *all* of Rodney's relationships strengthened. Friendships do not 'take' from one relationship and give to another, as in liquid ladled from a soup. Rather, strong, healthy bonding in one area adds more to the whole pot.

## SOLUTIONS

Men bond with other men through a variety of ways, some of which may seem odd to you. So be certain you examine his behavior and interests before judging them. Yes, hunting may seem barbaric to you, but it also may be a vital link for him to other men. So might be going to the Yankees game, or better yet, playing ball with his buddies.

- Don't feel rejected by his connection to other men, friends, *or* sports teams.

- Encourage him to keep his bonds with his friends. This will ultimately strengthen his connection to you.

- Don't allow all his time to be spent with others. Insist he balance watching the Bulls' game with time for you.

- Be sensitive to hierarchical issues with men. They are always there. This will be most exaggerated through his relationship with your father.

- Consider becoming a sports fan yourself. You may find a bond with him you'd not imagined.

*Gary L. Malone MD*
*And Susan Mary Malone*

# CHECKLIST
# UNHEALTHY BONDING:

1). Does he claim not to need male friends, maintaining no true adult relationships except with you?

2). Does he only see other men in terms of competition? If this is so, review Chapter Two.

3). Do his "nights out with the boys" seem purely for enjoyment, or does he seem to be avoiding you? I.e., do they pull the two of you apart?

4). Does he ever watch two consecutive three-hour football games, always on Saturday or Sunday? (Pull the plug!)

5). Does he continually "suck up" to other men, including his boss?

6). Does he still fight with his brother(s), even though both are well past childhood?

7). Is his life skewed in any one direction: work, you, alone time, male friends?

# CHECKLIST
# HEALTHY BONDING:

1). Does your man have meaningful friendships outside the bounds of your relationship?

2). Has he formed new friendships in his adult life?

3). Does he reminisce fondly of friends from his youth?

4). Are there out-of-doors activities (golf, camping, hunting, fishing, hiking, etc.) that he truly seems to enjoy and return from revived?

5). When out with his boss socially, is there a true sense of camaraderie?

6). Can he appreciate the importance of *your* outside friendships?

7). In spite of his healthy attachment to friends, if he had only one hour to spend on earth, would he spend it with you?

An emotionally healthy man will be able to keep a balance of maintaining peer contact while investing in his work, family, and especially, you. If he gives up all for you, he'll not likely be the same guy within a relatively short period of time. In other words, you'll have a hard time recognizing who he's become, and probably long for the man you met and with whom you fell in love.

## QUESTIONS AND ANSWERS

1). Question: My husband does not get along at all with his father, nor does he seem to have any close male friends. Are these two things related?

Answer: If a man has successfully conquered his own internal demons, he has the option to be friends with his father in adult life. The avoidance option is used because some men learn that they would not choose their parents as friends if they were not related. Men base future friendships on their interests and their experience—your husband *may* still be too conflicted about closeness to form friendships now.

2). Question: My boyfriend fights constantly with his brother. Both of these men are grown now, shouldn't they have outgrown this behavior?

Answer: Sibling rivalry, particularly among men, can be a lifetime experience. They should have grown out of it, but if not, it means they have not *each* mastered their own inner psyches and have some need to keep the feud alive.

3). Question: Four years ago, my husband's best childhood buddy died suddenly. Since then, he has shown no interest in maintaining old friendships or forging new ones. I know this isn't healthy, but what can I do?

Answer: After a time of grief and mourning, we *all* must learn to move on and embrace life. Your husband likely does not trust closeness due to his pain or may even feel it would be a disservice to "replace" his buddy. Offer an ear for verbalization and encourage him to keep living. As always, therapy may be his best tool.

4). Question: My man has a lot of female friends. Is this the same as having male/male relationships?

Answer: It depends upon how many is a lot, and more importantly, what they mean to him. People can relate person to person, but the sexual aspect usually has some impact. Be wary.

5). Question: After a night out with the boys, my man seems distant from me. Many of my girlfriends report this same behavior. If male bonding is supposed to bring us closer, what's going on here?

Answer: Your man may be feeling a loss by re-attaching to you after bonding with his friends. It means he's not learned to balance these senses yet in his mind. Perhaps some distance on your part after a night out will give him the space to ease back in. Of course, be certain he's really out with the boys! (See next chapter.)

6). Question: My husband has several relationships with men from work that he calls friendships. To me and my girlfriends, this male buddy-system falls way short of what we would call friendships. My husband disagrees. Who's right?

Answer: Men often try to believe they are experiencing closeness to colleagues when in fact they are simply in the *proximity* of these men. In the scenario you described, a man either does not make time for true friendships, or he overvalues the ones he has, often in a desperate attempt to stave off loneliness. Remember, too, women usually form tighter bonds in adult life than men (see the next book!).

7). Question: My boyfriend spends all of his time with his best friend, and even takes his side over mine. I'm jealous, but when I bring it up, my boyfriend says I'm too possessive. Do I try and change myself or him?

Answer: In any dispute, you must be the first priority. Respect his need for his friend, but if your relationship becomes a marriage, he must marry you, not his friend. Don't change yourself, and let your feelings be known.

8). Question: Quite often, my husband waxes fondly on how wonderful the camaraderie was on his college football team, and how much he misses those times. But he hasn't made any male connections since then, now that we're in the real world. Is this a refusal to grow up? Or is something more serious going on?

Answer: Usually this scenario exists because a man's relationships in adult life pale compared to the ones in his youth. The real answer is to quit living in the past and to find closeness now. I've personally been on many teams and enjoyed seeing my teammates, but never let that interfere with *this* week's activity. Again, encourage him to develop his life *now*.

9). Question: My husband's hunting trips have become more frequent and, with the stories they tell, little hunting actually takes place. I'm supportive of this manly thing, but I think this is just a front for partying.

Answer: I know of a hunting camp where you can hire someone to actually hunt for you while liquor and local women are readily available. Look deeper into your marriage (and into him) to see the source of the problem. Toxic hunting camps are not renewing for anyone and can, in fact, be dangerous. If he creates a cause to act out, this is a sign of something wrong at a deeper level.

10). Question: My husband stuck his stuffed fish right in our living room! I didn't raise a stink when the company sponsored the fishing trip, but *now* this animal shares my daily life. I have noticed however, when couples come over, the other men always seem in awe. What happens if I just misplace the ugly thing during the next cleanup?

Answer: Throw it out at your own risk! These trophies, as absurd as they seem to you and most women, are primitive connections to other men as well as an assurance of competency. If the job fails, he can always catch fish for you! Seriously, if you can tolerate the stuffed mount, it will do him worlds of good.

So, male friendships are indeed of vital importance to all men, encompassing a vast array of drives and conflicts within a man's psyche. Know, however, that no matter how lasting or close these bonds are, for a healthy male they cannot surpass those with a woman.

*Off Virgin Gorda, British West Indies:*
    *"Come about, hard port. They're gaining on us!"*
*We struggle with our sails, racing madly across the sparkling blue waves as the surf sprays over the bow.*
    *"It's a beam reach to Bitter Ends," our captain yells as we draw in the sheet. "I think we've got the angle."*
    *Just then, I look up to see our competing sailors. The boat contains two quite attractive couples in their thirties, all completely naked.*
    *"Hey, Madigan," I yell to my cohort as I drop the mainsail sheet. "I don't think they're taking this race as seriously as we are."*
    *We stare, sweating as the couples smile, wave, and cut past us toward the harbor.*
    *"Beam reach, my ass," he calls over the rushing wind. "Next time, we're bringing women."*

## Chapter Five
# The Fifth Key: Sex

*"This new magazine is about sex, because that's what men think about the most."*
—Hugh Hefner in an interview with Mike Wallace, circa 1955.

## THE UNDYING DESIRE

It will come as no shock to women to find that sex is the driving force in men's lives. Statistics say that a man thinks of sex at least once every sixty seconds. Again, few women would consider this a news flash.

Career choices, life paths, and living conditions along with choosing mates are all wrapped up in the man's psyche around sex. As Graham Nash of Crosby, Stills, Nash and Young said, "We didn't get into rock and roll for the money, we got into rock and roll for the women."

So while women's sexuality is more cyclical, circular, and wave-like, a man's tends to progress in a straight line. As Jean-luc Piccard, Captain of *The Star Ship Enterprise* was so fond of saying, "Engage."

Testosterone, laid down in the brain of the male fetus, marks the male psyche and is reinforced through psychological development and the maturing adolescent body. It is part physiology and part psychology. In the spinal cord of damaged men, the sexual impulse remains intact, even if the nerve pathways required to transport that impulse have been severed. Involuntary erections do occur—the body's own normal process. These two functions are just no longer in sync.

But male sexuality encompasses much more than mere physical sensation. And, as with the essence of guilt, it is the rest of this "stuff" that separates man from beast. Sam Keene summed this up in *Fire in the Belly*:

"...the penis is the straight and narrow pathway to paradise, the bridge over troubled waters we traverse to find the missing parts of our severed selves."

At the moment of orgasm during intercourse with a female peer, all conflicts are momentarily resolved in the male. Blissful merger with the primary love object occurs. Guilt is overcome or circumvented, and the object of infantile and adult romance is won. All anatomy is functional, undoing castration anxiety and assuring competency. Even a symbolic union with other men is reached, through attainment of *the* common goal. At that moment, the frost is on the pumpkin and all is right with the world.

Good grief, you say, all that happens with the climax of the sex act?! Where did this come from?

Biology provides part of the answer. Males need a high sex drive to insure competition among the fittest so that the biggest, strongest, and (eventually) smartest (or perhaps smoothest) man passes on his genes to the next generation. Psychology provides the flip side, in many ways following biology (Anatomy is Destiny), as man's mental life is built around his genitalia and sexual functioning.

Adolescence, after all, begins in boys with the first ejaculation (with women, it's the first menstruation). The sex drive in some form can then be found in virtually all of men's thoughts and actions.

A man's sex drive peaks between the ages of eighteen to twenty-five. It drops gradually for about ten to fifteen years, and then plateaus from forty to fifty-five. Here it drops somewhat but can remain relatively constant, absent disease or emotional instability. Men remain active into their nineties, if physically and emotionally healthy.

Women often find a man's seemingly unquenchable lust an irritant during same-age relationships while in the twenty-to-thirty age bracket. Often during this time they also have young children, adding an even greater strain, and widening the chasm between spouse's sex drives.

During the late thirties to early forties however, a woman's sex drive increases just as the man's decreases. This *can* result in a more blissful union with sympatic sex drives, combined with the man's increasing ability to tolerate closeness by this time.

The happiest marriages, however, are the fifty-plus ones, after the kids leave home. This removes the wedge in many relationships. Grandma was right— *after* the honeymoon, you wait until the kids fly the nest to really enjoy one another again.

Throughout life then, men's psychology stays wrapped up in their sexuality. All men like to think of themselves as good lovers.

> *"Can I move? I'm better when I move."*
> —The Sundance Kid.

## FANTASY: FROM EROTICA TO PERVERSION

> *"...A woman's greatest fear is being forced to have sex with a total stranger; this is a man's favorite fantasy!"*
> —Comedian Elaine Boozler.

A wide range of sexual expression exists in our world, and what some would call immoral or perverted, others see as simply individual tastes. Anything can be used as a defense—alcohol, drugs, violent behavior, pornography—but that doesn't mean that the *thing itself* is evil. The litmus test with sex, as with any substance or thing, is *how* it is used.

*Cabaret Royale. Dallas, TX:*

*"Jesus Christ, Deryl, at twenty dollars a dance, that woman's making four hundred and eighty dollars an hour!"*

*"Yeah," he answers smartly, "so who's exploiting whom?"*

*The experience is dazzling. Perfectly formed naked women prancing around us, smiling and acting oh-so-interested. Soon, I'm sixty dollars poorer.*

*Some of the women talk with us. Many are college students, making four hundred to six hundred nightly. Some of the more seasoned dancers, we learn, hate men, and many are gay. Life has finally presented to them the opportunity to extract payback from glassy-eyed fools with twenty dollar bills. It becomes clear that the sex here occurs only in the minds of men— true sex requires interaction. The dancing women serve only as stimulus.*

*Our interest and conversation soon drift to what we normally talk about: work, our wives, The Dallas Cowboys, our motorcycles. Suddenly a veteran dancer approaches from behind, placing her butt (in desperate need of a retread) on our shoulders.*

*"Lighten up, boys!" she says cheerily in a deep, east Texas drawl. "This here's a titty bar!"*

*She's right—this is supposed to be for fun.*

Quite often, women patients relate to me their fears, frustrations, and anxieties concerning this aspect of male behavior. Their emotions run the gamut. It all seems so baffling.

"I can't believe he went to that place," my patient says tearfully. An attractive woman in her thirties, she struggled to maintain closeness in her relationships, each man being somehow flawed.

"It's those jerks he goes out with. He only goes when they're around."

I attempted to discuss something about male bonding and the need for the illusions of reckless abandon, but she would hear none of it.

"How can I compete with those women? They're perfect!"

Ah, my opening. "He may do that for mindless entertainment, but he still chooses you. Besides, does he know how you feel?"

"Well, no," she admitted, wiping her eyes. "I guess I should tell him, shouldn't I. That's only fair."

I agreed and she left, the session ended. How ironic, that she felt so threatened by women with virtually no interest in her man. It is the fear of being imperfect, then rejected and abandoned that tortures most women. The irritation at her man is due to feelings of disloyalty and loss of attention, not from jealousy as no relationship takes place.

The question is, why do men *like* these places?

Clearly, if mutually gratifying intercourse with a female peer is the goal standard, what is happening at the *Cabaret Royale*, or the reading of *Penthouse*, or the sexual harassing that men engage in daily?

Male and female sexuality is not only *physiologically* different, but also *psychologically* so. Women can relate to Elaine Boozler's comment, "...And I don't *get* this restaurant called 'Hooters'. You sure don't see a restaurant called 'Peno's' for women. We wouldn't go!"

The differences between men and women in defining relationships was poignantly portrayed by Diane Keaton and Woody Allen in *Annie Hall*. As the couple inanely discuss issues of the day, their thoughts are typed on the screen for us to see: "I wonder if he likes me," Annie neurotically thinks, searching for affirmation. "I wonder what she looks like naked?" Woody's character lusts, his "little head" keeping priorities in order.

Normal male sexuality is difficult to define as the spectrum is fairly broad. What is clear, however, is that each man in his mind wishes to make love to as many females as is humanly possible. Men enjoy the role of the desired "Playboy" and like to view themselves as wild and free.

In 1966 and at the height of his playboy era, Joe Namath symbolically posed the question to all men: "Would you rather be young, single, rich, famous, talented, and happy—or president?"

As Ms. Boozler points out, visual stimulation is *much* more desired by men than women, as well as the wish to be "Top Gun." However, a healthy man can channel these desires to love only you. He may, as did Jimmy Carter, lust for women in his mind, but it is his behavior by which you judge him. In other words, contrast Carter with Bill Clinton, and the standards become obvious.

Varieties of normal sexuality must also be explained.

The issue of homosexuality will not be dealt with in depth in this volume, but we'll discuss it briefly here to help the understanding of male sexuality. The current controversy surrounding it centers upon genetic-versus-developmental factors. Boys go through a normal homosexual phase just prior to the Oedipal period, which may be exaggerated or diminished depending upon the person. True bisexuals are rare in adult life, as the conflicts aroused as well as the psychic energy needed to maintain this state are both enormous. Most bisexual men I have treated and known are simply homosexual and quite conflicted about it—again, another story altogether. Homosexuality *can* be a way to avoid the conflicts of genital sexuality with a woman. This, however, is usually transient and may or may not include actual physical, sexual encounters.

Men employ other ways of avoiding sexual conflicts with women as well. Anal regressions are common, particularly in pre-adolescents as the sloppiest boy or the one with the loudest fart is revered. For remnants of this in adult life, look into your man's garage (sloppy means full-flown regression. Extra neat means obsessive/ compulsive defense against sloppy. Okay equals relatively unconflicted in this area).

In psychoanalytic terms, a regression is just that: pulling away from and avoiding something that is more conflicted. A man fearing competency or guilt might choose to remain slovenly, driving off women and staying in the safe and familiar territory of anal matters.

The most common form of avoidance however, falls into the area of "perversions." Perversions provide pleasure through fantasies and behaviors that avoid the most conflicted act: genital intercourse with a female peer. Once the fears are overcome, this intercourse becomes the primary aim for men.

The term perversion gets a bum rap as we *all* have them in some way. The important thing is that genital sexuality predominates. Anything *less* is technically a perversion. In psychoanalytic terms, a perversion requires a *part* object (thing) and aggression (hostility). The "breast" of a woman "forced to dance" for you.

The growth industry in perversions is the dominating mistress, or Dominatrix. Look into the back of a *Hustler* magazine if in doubt. In fact, a recent interview with a practitioner from Houston revealed that most of her work involves S&M dominance at two hundred dollars an hour! Men secretly wish women to dominate them. What gives?

The "phallic" woman who dominates denies castration as the woman is no longer castrated.

Remember where castration fears started—from little boys seeing females with no penises. Now, she can be seen as having a phallus too. The man feels his genitalia are intact.

There is no performance anxiety, as the man stays receptive and passive—no performance required. This is not homosexuality (whew!) as the partner is a woman. And he attains closeness after orgasm. Guilt is also avoided as he doesn't even "screw like a man." The *Hustler* call girl said most of her clients, very macho types in real life, preferred to receive anal intercourse from her toys.

Sadism is the flip side of masochism. Men who express a need to dominate are often defending against a fear of incompetence *and* a wish to be dominated. Such men are readily evident. You don't need this.

Men whose *primary* sexual pleasure comes from magazines, movies, or girlie shows are garden-variety voyeurs—too chicken for the real thing. Of course, this is not restricted to men as women's strip bars and television commercials (the diet coke guy, remember?) proliferate today. Voyeurism, "attempting to taste the honey by licking the outside of the jar," is ultimately dissatisfying.

Don Juanism—the need for many women or simply hypersexuality (wanting sex all the time)—represents the relative stronger sex drive in men *and* a need to prove competence by activity.

The singles scene actually has heightened this behavior in both men and women. You can locate this evening's sex partner without even risking rejection or the entanglement of calling for a date! As Joe Namath said in a 1966 interview: "I don't like to date so much as I just like to kind of, you know, run into somethin', man."

No risk, no commitment, just sex. AIDS and our violent society have curbed this considerably. Even Broadway Joe stayed a monogamous family man for over fifteen years.

On the one side, Don Juanism is considered *almost* normal for men in the eighteen to twenty-five-year-old group (those with raging testosterone levels). Through this period, men wish for sex often and with many women. As Merlin said to Arthur's father on how to cross a chasm to his love in *Excalibur*: "Your lust will carry you." (He flew.)

On the other side, however, during and especially *after* this phase, this behavior is used as a primary defense to conquer many women in order to assuage fears of incompetency (i.e., castration anxiety). It can also be a counter-phobic way to ward off homosexual urges as well as override guilt and deny the need to attach to one woman. Healthy men give up the need to "have all women," and can put their energy into just one.

Also, a healthy man doesn't need sex every time he wants it to feel like a man. If a man *does* need sex to feel manly, he's using it as a defense. Healthy, intact men with a strong sense of self can live for long periods of time (if needed) without genital intercourse. The reasonable compromise is *your* choice.

So how much is too much? Sexual addiction has gotten a great deal of attention over the past several years, both in the popular and professional literature. Sex Addicts Anonymous has grown from a fringe group into a respectable 12-Step treatment model.

What is sex addiction? Isn't it just exaggerated Don Juanism? Well, that, and more.

Anything can be used to defend against or avoid anything else. The pleasure of sex can defend a person from the pain of separateness or emptiness. Hypersexual, or sex addicts, do not necessarily experience sex more pleasurably than we do. It simply occupies a place in their psychic lives that is key for defensive function and self-esteem regulation. (They are not biologically different either.)

The truly addicted male strives to undo past injuries or inadequacies through current conquests. Often, these men have been abused or overstimulated as children and this type of sexual activity as an adult provides a way of mastering the traumas. This behavior should *not* be tolerated in a relationship and *is* very treatable.

As with all addictions, the destructive behavior must be stopped and the underlying issues understood and worked through. Treatment is available. However, he will not go if you enable him by pretending all is well. Set firm limits. Be patient, however. This treatment is generally long-term and painful, but successful.

Some men treat women merely as sex objects. In this scenario, the woman serves limited functions to the man—sexual pleasure and assuring competency as well as undoing castration. Men have the ability to experience sexual gratification without really attaching, and this is exaggerated if other men are around. Relating to a real woman means allowing closeness and deeper attachment. This is threatening to men individually, and as a group. The pinup in the locker room is an example. Airbrushed and paper thin, she can't even speak, but is the object of great interest.

If a man can *only* relate to women as objects, you don't need him. He would be difficult to treat as well.

## INFIDELITY

Statistics show that seventy-five percent of married men have had extramarital affairs. The rate is almost as high for married women. In a land where our wedding ritual promises, "Forsaking all others ...till death do us part," what gives?

Again, let's digress a moment into the animal world.

More recent studies on infidelity focused *not* on the psychology or sociology of relationships, but on the evolutionary biology. Researchers looked to animal models to understand mating and monogamy, and to draw parallels to us: basically, we have *evolved* to be like this. They found that in most species, mated females are promiscuous and males are worse.

The authors studied bird pairs who "mated for life." Surprisingly, eggs raised by the pair often showed genetic differences from the male. While he roamed in quest of nesting material, his loving spouse accepted other males. Of course, our noble twig gatherer also had a wandering eye, and while out, mated with as many females as would accept him!

The end result provided a stable nest with two devoted parents who added variety and diversity to the gene pool.

Mammalian species showed a similar pattern, especially primates. A unit or home was established, and the female felt lust for the dominant male, while her spouse lusted for whomever was available. Considering our own DNA remains almost identical to the primates studied, no wonder monogamy proves so difficult!

Of course, the thing that differentiates us from higher primates is our capacity to reason coupled with the development of our superego—the faculty for guilt.

We also fantasize about events and anticipate outcomes. This helps as well as complicates our lives (you don't see neurotic, guilt-laden gorillas), as we can *choose* the behavior that is in our best interest.

Interestingly, during the '70s, a relaxed idea of marriage floated about. In the book *Open Marriage*, both members of a couple openly took lovers. The husband and wife co-authors subsequently divorced. The *desire* to mate broadly may be in our genes, but our psychology will not allow it.

The fantasy remains though. In the movie *City Slickers*, a neurotic Billy Crystal asked straightforward wrangler Curly if a beautiful woman could cause him to consider infidelity.

"Is she a redhead?" Curly asked. "I *like* redheads."

Infidelity does, however, continue to be the bane of modern relationships, with males outnumbering females in both frequency and duration of transgressions. Again, a man wishes to be attached, but then feels smothered, pushing away from the entrapping object. He wishes to prove himself competent and desirable with as many conquests as possible, tempting fate (and guilt) by seeking out the forbidden fruit. These wishes are present in all men, but a healthy man can make a commitment and stay with it, choosing the package of fidelity and completeness over physical and psychological gratifications that serve no real purpose.

Choose wisely and set your standards high. If not, you may enable this behavior. Always remember, it is preferable to be alone than be mistreated or abused.

*"Whistling in Amsterdam":*

*Why don't these people use vowels, I think, struggling with my map in the dim streetlight. My wife has remained at the hotel, a victim of jet lag, but I am too excited to sleep and search vainly for the "cultural district."*

*Nothing in my experience of growing up on the west side of Ft. Worth, Texas has prepared me for what lays around the corner. One of the most beautiful women I have ever seen sits virtually naked in her window, reading a book while eating an apple.*

*Is she cold? I wonder, snug in my ski jacket. Then I see her space heater. I am inclined to knock on her window and let her know she's forgotten to put her blinds down. Then, her gaze locks onto mine and she smiles invitingly. Am I psychotic from jet lag? I blink, half expecting a bologna sandwich and a chocolate milkshake to appear as perhaps I have fallen through the looking glass into a land of magical wishes.*

*To my surprise, I now notice all the windows on the street have beautiful naked women sitting in them. My culture shock eases. This is the Dutch version of the Chicken Ranch—commercial sex workers, they are now called. I smile sheepishly and turn back for my hotel. The Riek Museum can wait until daylight.*

Across all cultures, language barriers, and even within species, the sex drive remains the same; a central focus of our thoughts and feelings. Sharing no common language, the Dutch woman communicated volumes to me with a single glance. It is the language we all speak.

All men can relate to the ending of Larry McMurtry's *Some Can Whistle*:

"Their voices, like Jesse's now, had once all whistled the brainy, sexy whistle of youth and health, tunes that those who once could whistle too lose but never forget."

# CASE STUDY

*"Cancel my subscription immediately!"*
—irate mother of thirteen-year-old after receiving
the *Sports Illustrated* swimsuit issue
(this scene is repeated annually).

### Bill

Bill was a lady's man. Smooth and attractive, he prided himself on being able to attract and bed all varieties of women. The "nicely dressed wives in Volvos" were his biggest prize; the unreachable ones during his destitute, obese, high-school days.

Bill entered psychoanalysis after repeated attempts at shorter-term psychotherapies and medication management failed to touch his deep-seated depression and difficulty in regulating self-esteem. Psychoanalysis seemed his last hope as he remained lonely and depressed into his late forties, in spite of career success and a seemingly happy marriage to a young, beautiful woman. This marriage was, however, Bill's fourth, as each preceding wife had initially fulfilled him only to fall short and be pushed aside as defective. Fidelity was never seriously considered.

When he was quite young, Bill's parents had divorced, leaving him largely unattended during his childhood in a rough part of town. He liked to observe his older sister shower through the sideyard window, and was fascinated by the string of men his mother dated. Once he and a friend convinced a neighbor girl to pulls her pants down and he sold tickets to the show for a quarter.

His drive and intelligence earned him a scholarship to college and a business degree. His well-honed entrepreneurial skills brought distinctive success and experiences with women. Now fit and attractive, he took great pleasure in seducing as many as possible, forgetting them as soon as the conquest was achieved. His greatest pleasure was overwhelming a woman with his sexual prowess as she gasped, "Oh, Bill, you're too much for me!"

In analysis, he was evasive and narcissistic, missing often and ignoring the bill. What emerged however was a frightened, lonely man, fearing inadequacy and living the pain of early rejection. The fat, detestable boy from the east side of town who couldn't get a date stayed with him, and could only be temporarily appeased with a victory over those who injured him before.

Slowly his psychoanalysis deepened, revealing fears of being unloved, doubts about his manhood, and harsh primitive guilt, which could be circumvented but never completely avoided. His arrogance to me gave way to genuine attachment, realizing the chance to feel closeness without the need to win over a competitor.

However, he then began to feel unmanly around me, fearing I'd look down on him. One night he was unable to have an erection with his wife. He abruptly terminated his analysis, leaving a message with my secretary to send him the bill, which he never paid. I was the sixth therapist fired.

Bill's hypersexuality was a way to compensate for his long-standing feelings of incompetence and inadequacy. He could also substantially "pay back" those who had rejected him by reversing the roles— now, he was the rejecter. The victories were hollow and temporary as his deep-seated wounds could not heal. The cost to his personal life was enormous. With the pain of explaining the original injuries too great, he moved on. Six months later I received a referral request from a new psychiatrist (a woman) who he had sought for treatment.

The pleasures of sex for Bill were secondary; they were used to attempt to quell deeper pain, which never subsided.

Bill's case, of course, is an extreme example, but serves to accurately show how a man's deepest fears manifest in his sexuality.

## SOLUTIONS

Next to infidelity, women complain that their husband's sex drive drops *too* much, leaving them frustrated in their forties. First, be sure nothing is physically wrong (send him to a urologist)!

The second cause of abnormal decreased sex drive is emotional—the cardinal symptom of depression in men ("Can't eat, can't sleep, can't screw."—My first psychiatric professor). Often, decreased libido follows loss of potency as the years pass, affecting men in variable ways. Men most often enter therapy or analysis at this time.

- Accept that men's sex drive is different from yours. He will think differently from you and the other women you know.

- Sex should be a *part* of your relationship—not all of it or none. Monitor the balance.

- Men have the natural inclination to wander. Make sure he knows your position and the consequences if he chooses to go this route. Men most often stay faithful to prevent losing their attachment.

- Look but don't touch is fine for both parties.

- Remember: a man's sex drive drops off as his attachment increases. This can work in your favor over time.

# CHECKLIST
## UNHEALTHY SEXUALITY:

1). Is he an extreme—wanting sex either all the time or never?

2). Does he avoid sex, saying it's dirty or immoral? (see Chapter Three.)

3). Does he withhold sex from you, then satisfy his needs by other means? I.e., pornography, strip clubs, etc.

4). During times of normal stress (normal defined as not the life-altering kind such as death of a loved one, loss of job, etc.) does his sexual appetite vary drastically either way?

5). Does he make catcalls toward other women in your presence?

6). Is he sexually cold and distant and unwilling to talk about it?

7). Does he press you to play-out sexual fantasies with which you're uncomfortable? Are fantasies his *only* form of satisfaction?

# CHECKLIST
# HEALTHY SEXUALITY:

1). Does he accept your "no" without holding it against you?

2). Is sex only one form of intimacy between you?

3). Is he monogamous?

4) Is sex with you his most satisfying means of pleasure?

5). Is your sexual life varied—playful, loving, erotic?

6). Is he sensitive and attentive to *your* needs?

7) Even if he looks at other women, does he assure you by whatever means that you are the one he wants?

Again, sex is a central motivating force in the minds of all men. If you are the object of his affection, this is a good thing. Romance is, however, like a dance, and is most enjoyable when both partners are willing and in sync. You may have to help him know how to waltz with you.

## QUESTIONS AND ANSWERS

1). Question: My husband and I used to have a very satisfying love life. Now, however, he's become sad and depressed and our sex life has died. Is this normal?

Answer: No. It is, however, very common. Not only is depression treatable (see Chapter Six), but a man can lose sexual functioning beyond a certain age if he is inactive. You must encourage him to seek help.

2). Question: On nights out with his friends, my boyfriend sometimes goes to strip joints. He says it's nothing, but it hurts me nonetheless. What should I do?

Answer: If it truly hurts you, discuss it openly and frankly with him. He should choose your peace of mind over an activity he says is "nothing." Be aware, however, this activity *really* is nothing for most men. Explore your insecurities, but insist on being treated in a way that is best for you.

3). Question: My husband likes to engage in fantasies when we make love. While this doesn't bother me (I actually like it) I sometimes wonder if it means I'm not enough for him. Should I worry?

Answer: To indulge your partner on occasion can be a loving and giving act on your part. Make sure *your* fantasies get equal billing. If he seems satisfied with you overall, I wouldn't worry. Also, keep in mind no one ever fulfills another's fantasies one hundred percent, so don't make that your goal.

4). Question: I had dated my husband for two years before we married one year ago. Recently, I found pornographic magazines tucked away in the closet, and he confessed sometimes he still looks at them and masturbates. I'm devastated. I thought our sex life together was wonderful. Is it me? What should I do?

Answer: Approach this area carefully. If the pornographic material is just "spice" for him, it may be harmless and actually enhance your sex life. Remember, couples who on occasion masturbate separately make better lovers to their spouses. If it's too much, or *instead* of you, there may be a problem. Rest assured, it's not your inadequacies. Spend time with him to answer these questions.

5). Question: Recently, I found out that my husband of five years was having an affair. He has stopped it, and claims "she meant nothing," that it was just sex. Though I still love him, I don't know whether to stay in the marriage or leave. Will this happen again? Can I ever trust him? What should I do?

Answer: Affairs are common, but that does not make them acceptable. No affair "means nothing," and just what it *does* mean to him is the key. He must

Gary L. Malone MD

address the driving force in him to prevent it from recurring, combined with your stance on zero tolerance. Don't leave until he has a chance to respond and prove himself. Many marriages emerge strengthened by this experience. Trust him slowly and only after it has ended.

6). Question: My fiancé confessed recently (after much drinking and soul baring) that once in his early youth he had a homosexual experience. It's never happened again, and he swears he's not gay. Do I believe him?

Answer: Homosexual experiences are very common in adolescents and young adults when men are first experiencing their own sexuality. Look for evidence to the contrary and believe him if you have none.

7). Question: I can tell by my husband's reactions that sometimes other women turn him on. He always denies this, and says he just appreciates pretty women. Should I worry about this? Will he have an affair someday?

Answer: Your husband may be married and monogamous, but hopefully not dead. Any person can become aroused when in the presence of an attractive person of the opposite sex. Judge him by his attitude to you, his behaviors, and his commitment. Lusting for other women is really unrelated to cheating (again, compare Presidents Carter and Clinton).

8). Question: My husband has struggled with drug addiction for ten years. Last year, he got clean, but his desire for sex dried up with his disuse of drugs. What happened? Will his libido return?

Answer: This phenomenon is not uncommon, but must be taken seriously. He may be depressed, or used the drugs as a psychological or physical stimulant. Men who have abused find their libido decreasing in the early stages of recovery. Libido should return, but if it *doesn't* within six months, seek further help.

9). Question: Sometimes my boyfriend has bouts of impotence. Though he doesn't want to talk about it, is there anything I can do?

Answer: This is a sensitive matter and you don't want to make his castration fears worse by being indelicate. Impotence that is transient is usually psychological, whereas repeated bouts may be physical. Ask him to see an urologist if the bouts persist but make sure you support him in his approach to the problem.

10). Question: My husband prefers oral sex to any other kind. Is this normal?

Answer: Oral sex is enjoyable to a healthy man both in giving and receiving, but technically should still be foreplay to genital intercourse. Oral sex to orgasm occasionally is reasonable and a change of pace. If it is his *only* or most enjoyable activity, something else has come into play. Men who most desire receiving oral sex describe the feeling of power derived from this act.

If you include giving him oral sex in your lovemaking, treat it as a gift from you to him. It keeps the power balance clear. A man should want to please you also, but beware if he gets too much pleasure from the act of your receiving oral sex. It may represent a submissive fixation on his part.

11). Question: My man's sex drive is way lower than mine. Nothing is wrong with him physically or psychologically, his drive is just low. What do I do?

Answer: What you want to do is maximize your man's potential as your lover. If he cannot perform at the level that entirely meets your needs, you must ask if the whole package is worth it. If so, adapt. If not, there is no loss of honor for leaving a relationship that does not satisfy this need. Also, I've found that couples with drastically different sex drives often struggle, so bear this in mind while choosing.

12). Question: I live with a man who's obsessed with sex. How do I make this work?

Answer: As above, if his sex drive outweighs yours drastically, decide if he's the best match for you. Explore the obsession to see what it's really about. Often, a woman tells me her man is obsessed simply when he wants it more than she does. Remember, this is normal in age groups prior to the forties. And the next time you watch a bullfight on

TV, notice that the bull's raw aggression propels it forward. The matador's *knowledge* of the bull allows him to catch it. Use your red cape wisely.

13). Question: My husband wants me to watch pornography with him. It's sort of a turn on, but I'm concerned about why he finds this so exciting. He's pretty normal in all other ways, and seems really dedicated to me. Should I be concerned?

Answer: Many couples report this is enjoyable if it is a mutually shared wish. Decide if it's something *you* would enjoy and tell him. Actually, one way to add richness to monogamy is through shared experience. Enjoy.

14). Question: My new boyfriend is so conservative. He only knows *one* thing in bed. He's really sweet otherwise and I like him a lot, but I'm not the tender type—the guy is supposed to know what to do. Any thoughts?

Answer: Your boyfriend may be simply inhibited and have less experience than you do. If you really like him, talk frankly and offer encouragement. If he's really too inhibited to enjoy you, remember that Freud started an industry from people such as this—send him for treatment. As always, judge the whole package when deciding.

15). Question: I've recently had surgery for cancer and cannot have sex. My husband says he wants no others, but I know he has a normal sex drive. What should I do?

Answer: It sounds as if your husband truly loves you for who you are, with sex being only part of the package. His concerns for you outweigh his drives. Count your blessings.

## Chapter Six
## The Rule-Outs

*"There are no victims in adult relationships,
only volunteers."*
—Common wisdom.

For the sake of completeness, let's talk briefly about men who may be covered by our five principles, but suffer from some form of psychopathy. Not coincidentally, these men outside the bounds of normalcy comprise the relationship rule-outs—those unable to sustain a romantic union with a woman.

Sometimes of course these men are easily recognizable, as in the case of overt homosexuality, or one who sees flying saucers in the rear-view mirror. But often, they blend into the normal bounds of society, and women find themselves well into a relationship, having invested huge amounts of both time and energy, before the poison becomes apparent.

So, how do you tell if he's a stinker *before* you've bought the whole package?

Often, the answer is subtle. You can't know until some investment of time, energy, and often stomach lining has taken place. However, early warning signs exist that you can use to avoid painful, doomed connections. Education can help you keep from being the "jerk magnet" many women feel they have become.

Observe and experience your man in a variety of settings and stressors before committing. Love *may* be blind, but you don't have to be. This chapter will help you learn about the major areas of psychopathology that would "rule-out" a man from being a potential mate. As mentioned before, you will like yourself—and your life—better without being with one of these. Many worse fates exist than being alone.

## THE CHEMICALLY DEPENDENT MAN

*"Whiskey River take my mind."*
—Willie Nelson

A toxic man cannot effectively relate to a woman in a whole and complete way. Drug and alcohol addictions cause physical changes, as well as distort emotional and cognitive functioning to the point that only primitive attachments and "need gratifying" objects are sought out. In fact, most psychiatrists feel that a person who is toxic cannot benefit at all from psychotherapy until *after* he has detoxified.

Chemical dependence is now seen as a progressive, fatal illness, wounding all in its path, before finally killing the individual.

Along the way come pain and heartbreak as an alcoholic or drug-dependent person can be quite charming and exciting; often the "life of the party." Subtly, a woman in a relationship with an addict realizes that his capacity to recognize and meet her needs is impaired. As alcohol or drugs rob the individual of his emotional strength and ability to regulate self-esteem, you become a need-gratifying object—there only to serve. The chemical is the first and only love, excluding all others. Denial and rationalization are exquisitely honed to convince you all is well, even when you know it's not.

A typical case was presented recently with a man in his late forties, referred by his internist with liver enzyme elevation. A successful businessman, David was known for shrewd negotiation tactics. A drink sealed all deals, as well as providing stress relief for business setbacks. His loving wife seemed oblivious except when he fell asleep in front of the television even when company dropped by. This type of *faux pas* caused a stir, but since they had actually been estranged for years, not much of one.

In treatment, the patient's liver status become our primary focus: death in five years. He decided he didn't want to die. As recovery progressed, his wife noticed something surprising—the return of the man she had married so many years before. After intense and often painful couple's work, they reestablished the relationship they had lost over years of stress and toxic haze. At six months, David remains sober and his wife says they are still in their second honeymoon.

So, how can you tell "social drinking" from addiction? Apply a few simple principles.

A social drinker can limit to no more than ten drinks weekly or three drinks nightly for three months. I have never had an addict take this test and pass. If he can't do this while trying, he's got the *disease* of chemical dependency. Usually, if a person asks the question, he knows the answer.

There is no "social" standard for marijuana, cocaine, or hallucinogens. Beyond a certain age, *any* use is suspect. Most serious drug users are obvious and, hopefully, not a real consideration for you.

If you learn your spouse or mate is chemically dependent (this can develop later in life), what do you do?

Simply put: support him if he chooses to recover, exit quickly if he does not, and accept nothing less than abstinence.

This problem will *not* get better on its own, no matter how innocuous it may seem in the initial stages. There is no such thing as a "happy drunk" if the person is addicted.

Denial on your part can be every bit as strong as it is for the chemically dependent person. One reason for this is once you break through the denial and admit a problem does exist, you are left with decisions concerning what to do about it. By all means, seek help for yourself, help in sorting through the fact from the fiction, be it from a therapist, hospital, or support group such as AlAnon.

Chemical dependency is a *family* disease, affecting each member differently and the unit as a whole. **Never** assume the children don't know Dad's drunk every night, even if he's not stumbling. They do. And, they are drastically impacted by it. So are you.

*Recovered* addicts often make good mates. But an active user will break your heart as he kills himself slowly but surely. Only pain can result if you stay and you actually reinforce his perception that things are okay ("you're still here, aren't you?").

Don't be an enabler—both of you will be killed if you do.

## NARCISSISTIC OR SOCIOPATHIC MEN

*"C'est Moi!"* ("Is I!")
—Sir Lancelot

Narcissistic or Sociopathic men are often charismatic and externally successful. They attend to their own looks and present well. Their intuition often allows them to "read" you well, creating a sense of false intimacy. You are, however, only an object to be used in their minds for perceived gratification as they lack the capacity to truly love another.

In spite of its appeal as a love story, if Lancelot truly loved Guinevere, he would not have doomed her to the fate she received or deserted his friend's (Arthur's) dream. Narcissistic infatuation can feel like love but it is shallow and cannot last. The way to recognize this is by the early intensity (feels good but it's *too much*), followed by disgruntlement when the shiny new penny (you) loses its luster.

You may feel idealized and swept off your feet at first, but then realize you simply serve a need for him, and often not even as a real person. A man with this type of character pathology uses women to bolster his own psychic defects, rarely even experiencing you as a separate and complete human being. Watch to see if he *really* cares for your needs, and isn't just using his intuition to manipulate you. With most narcissistic men, you quickly become devalued so move slowly, watching for signs.

A sociopath will lie. Once this pattern emerges, set your boundary as quickly as possible and leave if he refuses to enter treatment.

I once saw a patient who came in three months pregnant, distraught and stunned. She had married a man after a whirlwind romance of less than six weeks, a man who on the surface appeared to be the answer to all her dreams. A successful, handsome doctor, he was attentive and kind. Even her mother liked him!

Then she noticed something strange—his call schedule seemed erratic, unlike other doctors she had known. Unfamiliar women called then hung up when she asked their names. She went to the hospital where he ostensibly worked only to learn the shocking truth—they had never heard of him! When confronted, he admitted the deceit (he sold stereos and presented as wealthy on credit cards) but wanted to stay married anyway. With a baby on the way and having quit her job, this new wife sought advice. Her husband agreed to therapy, but halfheartedly. Unfortunately, their therapy proved short lived, and I never learned their ultimate outcome.

Sociopathic disorders cross all cultural lines. Chairman Mao's recent biographer has given us a glimpse of the communist leader's character. Mao reportedly followed the peasant farmers' custom of not bathing—seeing it as unnecessary. He also didn't brush his teeth, rinsing his mouth at the end of each day with herbal tea to ensure cleanliness. He reportedly had a fine green slime over all of his teeth. In keeping with the principle: "For each according to their ability and to each according to their need," Mao developed a need to sleep with starry-eyed peasant girls.

Mao's physician informed him he suffered from a curable venereal disease, for which Mao declined to treat as it offered him little discomfort. It was reported that his young conquests bore *their* newly acquired infections with pride, as it was a gift from the Chairman. Beware of powerful men bearing the promise of connection with greatness, as *your* gift— be it physical or emotional—may "keep on giving" long after the encounters have ended. And like the confused, de-flowered, and now infected young peasant girls, you might realize that your role was simply to bolster his ego, and the impact on you was never considered.

A good narcissistic or sociopathic character disorder can weave an enchanting tale. If he seems too good to be true, he probably is. *Move slowly*— you will see all sides of his character over time. Do not volunteer to be taken advantage of. Narcissism and sociopathic manipulation cover deeper-seated psychic problems. The man needs (and can respond to) treatment.

## SADISTIC: MEN WHO GAIN PLEASURE BY PHYSICALLY OR EMOTIONALLY ABUSING WOMEN

*"She provoked me to hit her."*
—Abuser's excuse.

This should be a no-brainer, right? But my practice is filled with women who *repeatedly* seek out men who abuse them. This often stems from childhood emotional, physical, or sexual abuse, where a woman finds a man who treats her in a way that feels normal —just like at home. Remember, you tend to find a man who treats you the way you feel about yourself inside. If you hate yourself, it's easy to find a man who will enjoy hating you too. But, as Eleanor Roosevelt said, "No one can put you down without your permission." A woman must look into her soul to see why she has sought out such a man.

In her mid-fifties, Mary sat in my office teary-eyed. Her fifth marriage had just ended and the pain overwhelmed her. How could she have chosen the same man again? He had beaten her.

Seeking treatment for the first time, Mary finally saw her pattern. All her husbands seemed to truly love her. Subtly, after the vows were said, the domination started and then, the hitting. Bad luck?

Unfortunately, no.

Mary was the second of three children of a passive mother and violent, abusive father. While superficially loving, he would often belittle his children and, in violent fits of rage, beat them mercilessly. Mary blamed herself for these outbursts, and worse, learned to see her family as "normal." It was, after all, the only family she had ever known.

Mary sought out men who felt familiar, reminding her of home, which did have many warm and tender memories. She unconsciously chose men similar to her father, with violent dispositions. Mary was seeking out wife beaters.

Our work centered around her painful and traumatic memories of physical abuse with the terror, pain, shame, and rage that accompanied this. After many months of therapy, she came to terms with her past and saw how it affected current choices. A recent contact, now several years after our initial encounter, finds Mary seriously dating a quiet, reserved but loving man, with no history of violence.

If you find yourself in a violent situation, leave immediately. Take your children if you have them, and get out. *Then* delve into your own psyche. In other words, leave imminent danger first. Remaining in an abuser's life and bed only reinforces these behaviors and insures a repeat performance. Treatment is possible, but requires a high degree of motivation on his part and is long term and difficult at best. As my mother always said, "It takes two to tango." So see why you dance to this tune, then insist on another song.

An excellent description of the dynamics of both the abused and the abuser can be found in *By the Book*, a novel by my co-author, Susan Malone. Often women feel guilty or fear being abandoned or incompetent, which keeps them in the cycle of abuse. You must draw on your resources, and draw the strength and courage to act.

## SEXUAL PERVERTS

*"I can't stand to be with a woman after
I've fucked her."*
—Tony Roberts character
to Diane Keaton character
in *Looking For Mr Goodbar*.

About this subject, we can cut to the chase. What's he like in bed?

Morality (and disease) aside, you should know before you commit. A give and take with your man is healthy, but never do anything that you can't feel good about later. Fantasies in fact should be reciprocal (develop yours!), keeping in mind he should respect your wishes and concerns. A healthy man will be able to experience pleasure with you at *many* levels, with sex simply being one, albeit important, element. Be sure his most enjoyable act is genital intercourse with *you*.

But what if it's not? How much "healthy" perversion is tolerable? You be the judge. If your needs and his coincide, no one (including me) can cast stones. In an equal partnership, however, all partners needs are met, or at least negotiated, and no one submits purely to the wishes of the other.

One variety of perversion needs to be more fully addressed. The Whore/Madonna syndrome stems from a man with defective object relations (failing to fuse the good and bad objects) that persist into adult life. Once unfused objects are sexualized and affected by guilt, wild varieties can occur. You are one minute the object of unmitigated love and praise and the next, despised and disgusted. Rest assured, *you* have not changed so quickly. A man such as this may also have narcissistic or sociopathic character traits that often cover the oscillations in his mind.

Regardless, you don't need to be called an angel to feel good about yourself, and certainly don't need to be "dirt." Tell him to come back when he grows up and can treat *you* as an adult peer.

And clearly, if your man is a pedophile, a long-term relationship is likely impossible.

## PSYCHOTIC MEN

Hopefully, this is not an issue. You are not likely to date one, as men with serious psychotic illnesses have extreme difficulty with *any* closeness, particularly with women. Their internal thoughts and feelings blur into reality.

I have, however, worked with a rare few psychotic men who eventually learned to sustain a relationship with tremendous effort and support. But this is a long and arduous road, with the chances of success about one percent. The rule of thumb: if he sees flying saucers over the car on the first date, ask to go home. *Now*.

## TRAUMATIZED MEN

War veterans come to mind, but anyone who has undergone severe loss or physical and emotional abuse has internal traumas to be undone. These will come out in a depth relationship where our pasts always repeat themselves. Your support is essential, but therapy is really the key. Bear in mind that the abused may become the abuser later in life, and "identify with the aggressor" to undo the pain of being abused. Often, however, traumatized men become more sensitive and empathic and can be caring mates. As always, be certain of what you want and what you will tolerate.

A colleague of mine on the chemical dependency unit had been a Korean POW. He had enlisted at nineteen, brave and strong, and was captured when enemy forces overran his company. "We ran out of bullets," he said.

While held captive, he endured excruciating torture and watched many close friends brutally beaten and killed. After many months, he and a band of compadres escaped, reaching allied territory after a harrowing journey through the mountains. They returned home decorated war heroes.

Within ten years they were all hopeless alcohol and drug addicts. Many were dead. When not self-medicating with drugs and alcohol, they were plagued with the demons that come in the night—the torture that continued to torment their souls as they relived each beating, each murder. My colleague had seriously attempted suicide. Finally, the survivors helped one another seek treatment.

After a painful and difficult recovery, he met a woman unlike those he had known before. As he had known pain, he found he also knew love. Thirty years later, he still introduces her, beaming, as "my bride." Having seen the worst life has to offer, he treasures the warmth he found in this closeness. He knew how to inflict hurt and be hurt, and ensured it never happened to her. As with the ultimate paradoxes of life, the fact that he knew such pain meant she would know only joy.

## GAY OR BISEXUAL MEN

Gay men's psychological development is more complicated than straight men's. It is postulated that their biological brains may be different from conception (the counter-argument is that psychic homosexual development causes neuro-psychologic changes in the growing brain). Regardless, the complexity and controversies exceed the bounds of this book.

Straight women relate to gay men as friends—a less-complicated task than mates. But some gay men present as bisexual, and you need all of the facts. This seems easy enough. Even in the era of AIDS you need to test drive before you buy, which will answer the question. Keep your antennas up. There are few traumas as severe for a woman as when her man leaves for another man.

## THE DEPRESSED MAN

*"...Quoth the Raven, nevermore."*
—Edgar Allan Poe

Depression is the single most common psychiatric symptom and, the most treatable. Chronic depression robs a man of his self-esteem, energy, and motivation. Worse, he will likely look to you to "cure him" through nurturance. Why would you want this?

Often in the throes of new love, a man's self confidence rises and many flaws temporarily vanish, only to re-emerge when the flame cools. This is a rude awakening for many relationships. A chronically depressed man can experience his depression lifting with a woman's interest. Her attention undoes, temporarily, his own perceived deficits.

And though clinical depression is much more common in women than men, it strikes a high percentage of men nonetheless. A severely depressed man is easy to spot (it's unlikely you'd have more than one date with someone who talks to ravens), but certain women find themselves *attracted* to such men. This means you have rescue fantasies of loving someone out of his depression.

One patient repeatedly sought out obviously depressed men. She seemed to live to nurture wounded men back to health. Sadly, each man developed a passive dependency on her and her infantilizing attitude produced, not surprisingly, infantilizing behavior. Her efforts were often answered with men who resented her for her role in their plight. Only when she addressed her *need to nurture* (it was a way to heal her own wounds) was she able to make more reasonable choices.

Before investing, spend enough time to see what you'll have when the smoke of passion clears. A clinically depressed man cannot fully love, often experiencing you as a warm breast, and becomes a drain rather than a joy. Set limits, encourage and support, but be clear you are not on this earth (or in this relationship) to resolve *his* old conflicts, and direct him where this can be done.

Medications, psychotherapy, and psychoanalysis all are proven tools to deal with depression. Help him find the right one.

So, what if you've invested in someone who you *now* identify as a rule out? You should insist on and support psychiatric treatment, but set firm boundaries on how *you* expect to be treated. None of the disorders here are an excuse for someone to treat you badly.

You must also project to see if the outcome is worth the effort. Don't stay for neurotic reasons (i.e., guilt, fear of being alone). People do have the capacity for change, but motivation is everything and your limits can provide that motivation. If he doesn't try to change or is unable, **leave**.

This reiterates an important and oft-repeated point about relationships. Women's (and men's) need to be validated by having *a* relationship can override a person's judgment about *whom* they choose. Repeating old traumas in your adult life reinforces old beliefs about who you are and stifles change.

If your man truly is bad for you emotionally, you are much better off living alone than continuing the trauma.

This single point has the potential to alleviate tremendous external pain as I often see women fight to save a relationship that brutalizes their self-esteem and compounds their misery.

As we will discuss in the next chapter, the "right man" is not a mythical beast and can be found. Just remember: the wrong man can destroy your soul, stealing all meaning and joy from your life. You must learn to be comfortable alone before you can truly relate to another. Have courage. Choose wisely. Then act.

## Chapter Seven
# Finding Mr. Right

*"You've got to kiss a lot of frogs to find your prince."*
—Modern single women's lament.

Okay, how does this information help in real life? Having gone through all the points, are we discussing a mythical beast? *Only* if you accept anything less than a grand-slam home run.

After the overt rule-outs, you must balance all factors, modulating with some give and take, and make an educated choice. By knowing more about men, you can choose more judiciously, with an awareness of what the trade-offs are. Bear in mind, too, that contrary to popular belief, men do have the capacity to change (some) if there is sufficient motivation.

Enigmatic creatures, these men. They are often walking contradictions and paradoxes. But when the principles are grasped, they become understandable *and* predictable as well.

Men long to attach to a mothering object, yet deny this longing. If conflicted, they may over-attach at the expense of other needs or push away, sphinx-like, claiming to need no one. A healthy balance shows an ability to tolerate and seek out closeness without losing autonomy.

The fear of injury, symbolized by castration, remains a paramount force in men's psychic lives. They strive to display competency and dread encounters that prove them damaged or inadequate. "Pissing contests" among men help them see how they measure up and, hopefully, win. When they have been stung or injured, men seek redemption, which may prove a lifelong task.

"Anal regression," messiness, or its opposite, compulsive neatness, may defend either of the above. A healthy expression of this behavior is tinkering, which can also be useful (especially if the toaster is broken).

Guilt dominates men's thinking, particularly in adult life as they strive to win while avoiding their own internal retaliations for obtaining the taboo prizes. Rules and the like (commandments) serve as tools to circumvent guilt. Beware the guiltless, or sociopathic man.

Men need each other. They must overcome their overt competitive drives and fears of "losing" to connect, but without their friends, men are lonely. The tribe no longer gathers for the hunt, but the call is present in all men. Encourage the men around you to answer this call, and to maintain relationships with friends.

Sexual fulfillment is a prime source of enjoyment for men and women alike, but is more intense and focused in men and means more psychologically. Inhibitions and perversions are the extremes, but expect your man to primarily fulfill himself through genital intercourse with you. Make sure you like it too (or see your *own* therapist).

Attachment, castration, guilt, male bonding, and sex—yes, complicated creatures, these men. But understandable *and* predictable. Our categories only cover eighty percent of their behavior, the rest comes from their own idiosyncratic experiences. Get to know him to learn the other twenty percent. And the math is correct—you can learn one hundred percent (or close to it) about your man, and unravel the mystery of the ages for yourself. Knowledge *is* power. Use it wisely and to your advantage.

Does the *right* man for you truly exist? A man without the major rule-outs, and with enough health and intent to make you his mate? Yes, he does.

He might be sitting on the couch watching the ball game as you read this. As all men are potential murderers and rapists, all men are also potential good choices. You must simply get clear on what it is that you want, choose the best from what is available and adapt, or, help him change the parts that are not acceptable. Again, if no one meets your criteria, work on yourself and wait—a bad choice is never as good as being on your own.

In my work with addictions, the Serenity Prayer says volumes: "God, grant me the serenity to accept the things I cannot change, the courage to change the things I can, and the wisdom to know the difference."

The psychoanalyst puts a slightly different slant on the same theme about healthy adaptation by stating that a person confronted with conflict has three choices: 1). Change things in your head (perceptions, attitudes, unconscious conflicts); 2). Change things in your environment (remove the thorn, ask to be taken home); or 3). Leave.

What you don't do is accept a bad situation if other options are available. And if you look and study and plan, *other options are always available.*

A major impediment to finding a man for many women is a deep-seated resentment, or even hatred, for having been burned, sometimes repeatedly, by a man or by men in general. Anger and rage are healthy, burning clear the underbrush so that new growth may occur. Hatred, however, is like acid, scarring the vessel that contains it far more than the intended object. Resentment is akin to drinking poison in order to kill someone else.

If you have been betrayed, or abused, a healthy rage is useful—it can be the stimulus for introspection or the motivator to move on. Remember, the opposite of love is not hate; it is indifference. Once you *truly* don't care for him, you're ready to move on. If the hatred continues to smolder, it's not about him. He has simply plugged into your deeper-seated fears and insecurities.

Keep in mind: "Time wounds all heels." If he *really* is a jerk, your reflection is not necessary. Clean your own closet before seeking a new man and don't carry baggage into the new relationship. Be aware that just because one man (or many) was a creep, not *all* men are. Only after you've taken your own moral inventory and worked through your "stuff" can you choose wisely.

If the pool of your consciousness is clear and your line sits in the water with no nibbles, remember the old saying: "Only the person at peace with himself can enjoy the gift of leisure."

Find peace, be available, but be patient. Enjoy the gifts you have in the now with a watchful eye on your hook. If the one on your line doesn't measure up, help him with his shortcomings, learn to adjust, or release him and cast again.

Nothing will run off a new man quicker than the feeling that you are angry with men, or, a dreaded "man-hater." Do *your* work first.

Wisdom then lies in knowing where, with whom, and in what way to choose your battles and when to accept the inevitable. We all have limited physical and emotional energy and must choose wisely and well where to invest. Hopefully not by beating our heads against "things we cannot change."

When applied to relationships these adaptive guides can get skewed. People often lose their powers of observation and reason when falling in love (akin to becoming "enchanted" in fairy tales).With the right person, this is a mindless and almost mystical state of being.

So, what is love?

Love is: the realization of the early wished-for love object in adult life lived through your spouse; when a person meets your physical and psychological needs better than any other available person; the merger with your Jungian soul mate; a spiritual union with the one chosen for you before you were even born.

Love is all of these things.

However, love is *not* "never having to say you're sorry." Owning up to personal responsibility is vital to any relationship, but especially in the intense parameters of romantic attachment.

Love requires so many descriptions because it is indescribable. Any simple explanation is inadequate. It varies in quality between parents and child, siblings, friends, or spouse. Romantic love changes over time and life phase, each exposing dramatically different aspects. Love may be enduring, passionate, or simply warm and cuddly.

But how do you know it's enough or right?

A few lucky people do meet their soul mates— likely a similar psychological match with whom one can experience closeness and remain passionate. The overwhelming majority of us, however, must fill the bill as completely as possible and then accept compromise. Even the four parts of an adult couple (friend, companion, lover, and co-parent) will change in intensity and degree over one's lifetime.

In assessing a marriage or couple, I always ask both members the basic question: Is this a hopelessly damaged union that needs help in being disentangled, or is this a "good fit" with "bad stuff" in the way? I am very *pro*-marriage and *pro*-family, but find it a disservice to encourage a bad match to stay together. Divorce is rough on kids, but *much less destructive* than a toxic marriage.

I am convinced that each participant in a marriage must feel a romantic, almost mystical "something special" for his or her spouse. This likely, in fact, is a reliving of early life wishes, but remains at the heart of a solid marriage. If he doesn't stir your heart, you are probably better off alone. If nothing else, it provides the motivation to work at and for the union.

As Joseph Campbell said, marriage is an ordeal. It is "the submission of the individual to something superior to itself." Therefore, the sacrifice one makes while in it is not a sacrifice to the spouse, but to the relationship.

The tricky part being that about the time you begin falling in love is exactly the point where you are learning new and previously unknowable things about his character. In other words, as you drift into blinded bliss you need your powers of intuition and rational judgment the most.

Biologists say that love exists to insure the perpetuation of the species at the time that flight would be a more rational choice. Conscious awareness of you and your partner becomes the best tool, and backing out prior to imminent catastrophe is no loss of honor. But how do you judge?

I often hear women cite the relative man shortage as an excuse not to try. Contrary evidence lies in the experience. I've yet to work with a woman who desired a relationship and *didn't* eventually come across an acceptable man.

Be aware that as the years go by and passion wanes, character endures. Look for someone with whom you click emotionally. The best marriages are between friends.

The old rules of dating apply no matter what your age. Initially, date many men in a variety of social settings. This breaks down rejection jitters and improves social skills. Usually one or two make the initial cut and deserve increased investments of time and energy. A boyfriend is established when he is your only regular date.

As powerful as the urge may be to be swept off your feet, it is essential to keep your wits about you and remain objective. Of course, enjoy the mindless bliss of the moment, but this is the time to judge just with whom you are dealing.

Here begins the opportunity to learn about "him and you." Each of us relives our emotional history in love relationships. Aside from the obvious of how you feel, pay careful attention to his reactions to you as his guard drops. The following list is a compilation of ideas from previous chapters, and can help organize your thinking.

# CHECKLIST
# (KEY FOLLOWS)

1). Does he become needy and dependent, experiencing you as "Mom"?

2). Or, can he attach to you and still maintain his autonomy?

3). Does he push you away, feeling an obvious threat by your closeness?

4). Or, is he drawn to you while keeping some time to himself?

5). Does he remain distant and unattached, even though he has an obvious wish to be with you?

6). Or, when he becomes distant does he come back and explain why?

7). Since committing to you, have other drives gotten in the way of being close to *you*?

8). Or, does he have a healthy balance of all drives?

9). Does "sharing power" with you as an equal partner make him feel unmanly?

10). Or, after an initial power struggle (remember, he is a man and his first impulse is to dominate. It's how he deals with that impulse that's important) have you settled into an equitable relationship?

11). Does he need to push you away to assert his independence?

12). Or, can he be his own man while remaining close to you?

13). Does he show you off in public then neglect you at home?

14). Or, is he proud to have you on his arm *and* makes sure you know it behind closed doors?

15). Now that he "has you," does he seem guilt ridden or preoccupied with "doing the right thing"?

16). Or, does he feel gratified and proud that *you* love him?

17). Does he relish (or abhor) "living in sin" as preparation for marriage?

18). Or, is it you and the relationship between you that takes priority over convention?

19). Does he seem to fear "winning too much," self-sabotaging his career, status, or home?

20). Or, does he accept his successes as hard-earned and justified?

21). Is he fervently seeking redemption?

22). Or, does he seek merely, as George Foreman said, the *opportunity* to redeem himself?

23). Does he "flee" to spend time with his male friends just when you seem the closest?

24). Or, does he remain "there with you" during those times of deep bonding?

25). Did he renounce his male friends, saying he needs only you?

26). Or, is his main priority you, while still maintaining his friendships?

27). Was his father a god or a goat, a judge or MIA?

28). Or, does he now see his father as an individual, human being?

29). Has he become preoccupied with sex?

30). Or is sex just one vital *part* of your lives?

31). Does he insist on acts that make you uncomfortable?

32). Or are both of you comfortable in acting out your fantasies?

33). Does he avoid sex—looking blissfully content eating Oreo's on the couch?

34). Or can he find contentment in *both* these things?

35). Has he become preoccupied with other women, either real or imaginary (celebrities, etc.) since investing in you?

36). Or has his appreciation for other women (remember, men *are* very visual) remained about the same?

37). Does he treat you "too well," leaving you to wonder what's in it for him?

38). Or, is there a normal ebb and flow of emotion within your relationship?

39). Do you feel as though your own needs do not exist except as they relate to the relationship?

40). Or, is he interested in you as a person, and not just for what you do for *him*?

41). Has drinking or drug usage ever interfered with your life together, or his job, family, home, or other interests?

42). Or, does he just drink socially?

43). If he's a recovering alcoholic/addict, is he looking to you to fill that void?

44). Or, has he been clean and sober for at least one year before you began the relationship?

45). Does he put you down emotionally?

46). Or, does he honor you for being you?

47). Has he *ever*, even in the heat of the worst fight, even come *close* to hitting you?

48). Or, does he express his anger by acceptable means and get over it?

49). Does he try to control you in any way?

50). Or, does he validate your judgment?

51). Are you consistently an angel then a Jezebel?

52). Or, are you seen as a flesh-and-blood woman?

53). Is he convinced that someone or something is "out to get him," and acts from this place?

54). Or, does he have clear boundaries as to his own responsibility for his life?

55). Has he been severely traumatized, in childhood, in war, through anything, and not been treated for it?

56). Or, has he worked through his traumas enough to be aware of his emotions and explain them to you?

57). Has he ever had an ongoing homosexual experience, though now proclaims to be hetero- or bi-sexual?

58). Or, are his sexual affinities confined to women?

59). Does he show signs of chronic depression—can't eat, sleep, or have sex?

60). Or, does he merely "get the blues" now and then?

61). Do you sometimes find yourself wondering if life in a nunnery is all that bad? (A healthy fantasy, but in reality the food's lousy.)

62). Or, do you trust, respect, *and* love your man?

# SCORING

A "NO" answer to the odd-numbered questions is worth one point, a "YES" answer to these is worth zero.

A "YES" answer to the even-numbered questions is worth one point, a "NO" answer to these is worth zero.

Out of a possible sixty-two points, a score of zero to twenty means get out as quickly as you can pack your stuff! There is no room for discussion here.

A score of twenty-one to forty-one means you're on pretty shaky ground. Are all of your zero-pointers in one area or are they spread around? If in one area, you're probably dealing with a deep-seated fear, which the two of you alone won't be able to bridge. Insist on therapy. If this is refused, leave.

Also, if in this range, are your answers on the higher end? Use this as a barometer. No matter where you sit in this grouping, know that you're facing an uphill battle.

A score of forty-two to sixty-two means your relationship is probably workable. Again, if it's in the low range, reassess, negotiate, discuss, perhaps enter into couple's therapy. If it's in the upper areas of this grouping, you're on very solid ground. Count your blessings!

Of course, this quiz simply gives you some direction in regards to understanding your man. The best way is to *ask* him. Flat belly and a sense of humor aside, women most often tell me they want a man they can talk to.

Be persistent as this comes unnaturally to most men, but believe me, they have the ability to do it. You can help by asking about things that interest or bother him, such as is his team likely to make the playoffs or how his boss is treating him. Men complain that women mostly wish to talk about themselves, so show an open interest in *his* problems and triumphs. You can teach a man to talk with you.

Again, *any* man is capable of changing a great deal if he is motivated. This may simply require persistence on your part, or therapy. The real judgment usually comes when a woman threatens to leave if things don't change (*never* bluff). Many men enter therapy and greatly benefit from treatment via this route. If he shows no capacity to respond to your concerns or will not enter treatment even at the threat of losing you, then strongly consider leaving. Again, living independently is *much* healthier than living in a relationship where you feel "one-down."

So, what if after all the time and effort, Prince Valiant turns out to be part toad? It is your call whether the frog part's fixable, or, something to which you can adapt. Remember, you are responsible for acting in *your* best interest only, meaning you should choose the best available match, realizing that no man is all prince and no toad. Obviously, if he is primarily toad with no motivation to change, let him go. Reinvest in yourself and wait for the next opportunity.

Remember, no man is an island—he wants and needs a loving relationship as much as you do. Whether or not he is capable of sustaining that is the central theme of the story.

Patience, tolerance, and diligent work on yourself, then working together, is the best way for the two of you to evolve into a loving union.

And know, whether he is now able to show it or not, most men identify with Humphrey Bogart in *Casablanca* when he says:

"Someday, it may be tomorrow, it may be a week or a month, maybe even a year, but someday you'll realize how much I love you…

"Here's lookin' at you, kid."

# *Conclusion*
# THE FIVE KEYS

*"Once upon a time, I dreamed of becoming a great man. Later, a good man. Now, finally, I find it difficult enough and honor enough to be—a man."*
—Edward Abbey, *A Voice Crying In The Wilderness*

**The First Key:** *Attachment and Loss*

All men need to attach to a woman. This is largely unconscious and often denied. Men often fear the power of their own dependency needs, and therefore avoid these feelings.

**The Second Key:** *Mastery, Competency, and the Fear of Castration*

Men share a basic anxiety concerning injury based on a childhood fear of castration. They constantly seek to prove their manhood by affirming competency.

**The Third Key:** *Guilt*

Men are plagued by guilt. This is also largely unconscious and only emerges when internal transgressions occur.

**The Fourth Key:** *Men's Need for Other Men*

Men need other men. This occurs directly through relationships, and vicariously through identifications with sports teams and heroic figures.

**The Fifth Key:** *Sex*

Sex is a more powerful drive in men than in women, and directs most of their thinking.

# Epilogue

*"I'm living on things that excite me/be it pastry or lobster or love."*
—Jimmy Buffet.

And so, what is life? …

*"Life is bliss."*
—Airport Moonie, handing out pamphlets while wearing a "Hi, I'm from Mars," grin.

*"It restates the existential angst of non-being as it relates to the nothingness and negative entropy of the Universe."*
—Depressed patient's reaction to The Dallas Museum of Art's permanent collection.

Or:
*"You're born, you go on some diets, you die."* — Opus, Bloom County comic strip.


I have spent my adult life studying the internal workings of the human psyche, bringing into conscious awareness unconscious feelings and thoughts. And while Opus's sentiment is true, it's the going "on some diets" part that encompasses the vastness of our experiences.

Life is composed of choices, both external and internal. It can, indeed, be filled with the "existential angst of non-being," or can conversely be "bliss." Our realities begin and ultimately end within our own psyches. Which paths we follow inside our own minds and in our lives are entirely up to us. If followed true to our own spirits, the pleasures and joy will far outweigh the pain.

*Now I am the father and find myself struggling to keep up, my daughters' youthful enthusiasm carrying them over the sunlit reef. They squeal with delight at each brightly colored fish; pursuing down into the corals; looking like fish themselves.*

*I descend to bring up a King Conch for examination, its camouflage hiding it from less-experienced eyes.*

*"Cool, Dad," they signal with the thumbs-up sign.*

*The most ancient of cycles repeats itself within my family and the experiences of a lifetime ago are passed on. Perhaps a generation from now they, too, will feel a tug on the shoulder when it is their time to swim out to the reef.*

P.S. From Sally and Jill: "Sappy dedication, Dad."

CPSIA information can be obtained at www.ICGtesting.com
Printed in the USA
LVOW040711130312

272832LV00001B/7/P

9 781928 704003